ZORA!

▼

Zora Neale Hurston:
A
Woman
and
Her
Community

ZORA!

▼

Zora Neale Hurston:
A
Woman
and
Her
Community

Compiled and edited
by N.Y. Nathiri

A publication of The Orlando Sentinel
Sentinel Communications Company
Orlando/1991

For information write:
Bethany Mott
Sentinel Books
P.O. Box 1100
Orlando, Florida 32802

Jacket design by Clay Rivers
Jacket photograph by Frank Busby
Book design and page layout by Eileen M. Schechner

Printed in the United States by R.R. Donnelley

Library of Congress Catalog Card Number:
90-63868

ISBN 0-941263-21-5

Zora Neale Hurston,
who possessed the magic of words and a
complete understanding of Eatonville's
uniqueness, translated the African-American
cultural experience into stories with universal
appeal. To her, the historic Eatonville
community owes a debt of gratitude.

▼

ACKNOWLEDGMENTS

▼

This book about Zora and her community could not have been published without the dedication and support of a number of people.

To Zora's nieces and nephews — Winifred Hurston Clark, Edgar Hurston, Zora Mack Goins, Vivian Hurston Bowden, Dr. Clifford J. Hurston, Jr., and Lucy Hurston-Hogan — I am deeply indebted. For the help I received gathering family photos and memorabilia, and for their cooperation in every phase, I would like to especially thank Winifred Clark, Edgar and Clifford Hurston and Lucy Hurston-Hogan. From my initial meeting with Lucy in the summer of '89 and my subsequent introductions to other family members, I have relearned an important lesson: Don't believe the negative things people say about others. Contrary to what I had heard, Zora's relatives cared about her and wanted to do all they could to see her assume her rightful place in history. Without their willingness to share, a very important part of the story would have been left untold.

I could not have written the epilogue to John Hicks' masterful magazine piece if not for the dedication, nay the detective work of Cynthia Hart Scales and Marjorie Alexander Williams, two Fort Pierce natives. Knowing I was working on this project, Ms. Scales, a colleague of mine at the Preserve Eatonville Community office, began asking me questions, identifying names and telephone numbers of people she knew in Fort Pierce and making calls to them on my behalf. Marjorie Williams picked up where Ms. Scales left off. It was through her efforts that I was able to get access to the community. Over weeks, we talked; she did so much legwork, I kidded her that this had become her project. And when I returned to Fort Pierce, she accompanied me around Zora's old neighborhood, took me to the grave site and went with me to talk to those who had agreed to be interviewed.

The phenomenon that Eatonville represents has, for so long, been unknown, and there are precious few scholars and researchers with first-hand knowledge of towns established by people of African descent. Dr. Eleanor Ramsey and Everett L. Fly are two of the best. Conquering the restraints of time and prior commitments, Dr. Ramsey pushed to put down on paper the information we so desperately need to read. To my colleague in preservation, Everett Fly, my debt is ongoing. A professional of impeccable credentials, he has gone the extra miles to assist Eatonville in its quest for formal recognition of its heritage.

Thelma J. Dudley is another contributor whose assistance I had no right to expect. To say that Mrs. Dudley is busy is a gross understatement. A full-time doctoral student, she maintains national and international obligations to her church. She is the prototypic active, involved senior citizen. She truly extended herself to accommodate my needs; I am deeply appreciative.

To Alice Walker, my gratitude ever grows. From the beginning of our efforts in Eatonville, she has followed our saga, contributing at every critical juncture. She is constant.

Years of love and friendship helped me work my way through my personal essay. For the first time, I was called upon to examine my origins, to look at how I've become who I am. My mother, Ella Dinkins, responded in the perfect way to my questions, calling back any number of times to give me additional information as she understood my need to piece together circumstances or events. Careful not to represent only her perspective, she provided me with others that might be able to confirm or amplify what she had told me or given me to read. Louise M. Franklin and her brother, Augustus W. Franklin, are history buffs who appreciate the preciousness of Eatonville. Each provided access to information they knew would help me. To the congregation of the St. Lawrence A.M.E. Church, to Harriett Moseley, to Mary Montgomery and her daughter, Doris Bennett, I express appreciation for the use of material that shows the vitality of the Eatonville community.

Likewise, thanks to Dr. Delores Inniss, principal at Hungerford Elementary School, and to Sarah Jane Turner, principal at Wymore Career and Education Center, for their assistance illustrating Eatonville's proud legacy of education. And to Mayor Ada J. Sims, I say thanks for allowing your staff to assist me.

Over the years, I have been fortunate to work with a number of people whose professional standards are high, whose equilibrium does not waiver, even under the most stressful conditions, whose sense of goal permits them to achieve. In my relationships with Dixie Kasper, Bethany Mott and Eileen Schechner, my Sentinel Books colleagues, I have again found these qualities. I must say something more. I can find no fault with my editor, Dixie Kasper. She treated my every word with absolute respect, explaining every change she thought should be made, and never tampering with the integrity of meaning.

To the Preserve Eatonville Community board of directors — Eddis T. Dexter, Paula M. Gardner, Frank M. Otey, M. Jackie Perkins and James A. Shortess, I say thanks for your vote of confidence. And to the volunteers — especially Valada Flewellyn — who "minded the store" so I could complete this project, I could not have done it without you all.

And finally to Asili, my husband, Muhammad and A.Y., my two young men, Iyesha, my very precious little girl, and my dear, dear Mama, Ella — I say thank you for bearing with and supporting me through yet another challenge.

— N.Y. Nathiri

CONTENTS

▼

Discovery

1

Reunion

57

Celebration

77

Understanding

103

Discovery

Zora's interest in anthropology blossomed at Howard University.

DISCOVERY

▼

by N.Y. Nathiri

During the 1987 fall semester, I was on the road Mondays, Wednesdays and Fridays, driving from one end of Orlando to the other. A part-time instructor at Valencia Community College, I had pieced together a teaching schedule on both east and west campuses in an effort to earn a little more money. To pass the drive time, I usually listened to the local radio talk show.

One morning, the guest was "Stumpy" Harris, a partner in the law firm, Gray, Harris & Robinson P.A., and a former condemnations attorney for Orange County who was explaining the rights a landowner has should the government wish to take property. A citizen must receive a fair price for the land being condemned for public use; and if the landowner were not satisfied with the offer, he or she could take the government to court — at the government's expense. Why such a dry subject, I wondered. Then I remembered Orange County was in the throes of development and road improvement projects were under way all over the county.

As I turned into the college's parking lot, I clicked off the radio and pushed the interview into the recesses of my mind.

Some weeks later, my mother, Ella Dinkins, mentioned to me again that the county was considering a road project that would take some of her land. She had received the notice advertising the third hearing. Sick during the first, and out of town for the second, she had followed events by talking with neighbors who had attended. The project seemed inevitable. I suggested we make an appointment with Harris.

On a Tuesday evening in November, Mama and I, along

with Forrest Fields, an attorney with the Harris firm, and about 50 residents from Eatonville and Maitland gathered in the cafetorium at the Wymore Career and Education Center to hear the county's report. The engineers were direct: They would recommend to the County Commission that it authorize the widening of Kennedy Boulevard/Lake Avenue (the stretch of road bears two names — through Eatonville, it is called Kennedy Boulevard; in Maitland, Lake Avenue) from Lake Destiny Road east to U.S. Highway 17-92 from two to five lanes. This 1.3 miles of road improvement would cost $7.3 million. It would cut the Eatonville community in half; it would place four retention ponds on the east side of the town, destroying the Municipal Park; it would bring through the center of town 11,000 additional cars each day. There was not a single amenity or safety feature included in the recommendation.

I was stunned. I had come to the meeting fully prepared to accept the county's need to take some of our property. We had been through highway improvement before. Thirty years earlier, when Interstate 4 had been built, its construction took 7.5 acres of the ten acres we owned. As I sat listening, the enormity of the situation became painfully clear. If this plan were accepted, the Eatonville community would be destroyed. The oldest incorporated municipality founded by African-Americans would no longer exist as it had for more than a century. This town — known and loved by millions because of the writings of Zora Neale Hurston — would degenerate into a shortcut for travelers who wanted to shave five minutes off their drive time.

The County Commission would meet the following Monday. Eatonville's fate rested in their hands. That Monday, the chamber was packed. The commissioners were unanimous. Kennedy Boulevard/Lake Avenue would be widened as recommended by the engineers.

I was awash with emotion. I couldn't believe what I had heard. Eatonville had just enjoyed a very highly publicized nine months celebrating its centennial. Media from around the country had featured stories about the historic town and its most famous citizen, Zora Neale Hurston. How could the commissioners disregard Eatonville's historic significance? Why was it so necessary to work on this 1.3-mile stretch of highway? What were the real reasons?

There was no doubt in my mind that this decision had to be contested.

Until the commission passed its resolution to widen Kennedy Boulevard, I had no idea just how intense my feelings were for my hometown; nor had I realized how important my upbringing was to the person I had become. That November marked a turning point in my life. I have since come to appreciate the richness of my heritage, the specialness of the Eatonville community, the influence Zora Neale Hurston had on the shaping of my world view in ways I probably never would have realized if Eatonville's existence had not been threatened.

The cornerstones of my upbringing in the Eatonville community rested on family, religion, education and civic pride. From this foundation, I developed self-confidence, a desire to achieve, and a strong sense of security as a member of a community.

I can trace my family's Eatonville roots to my mother's mother, Addie Mae Gramling, originally from nearby Sanford. Of six children, the only daughter of Oscar Gramling and Ella Stone Gramling, MaMa was born in 1890 into a life of privilege. Her father, the proprietor of a

As teenagers, my grandmother, Addie G. Johnson and her brother, Albert, dressed in the latest turn-of-the-century fashions.

Courtesy of Ella Dinkins

barber shop whose clientele was exclusively white, owned one of the few houses in Sanford with indoor plumbing. MaMa attended Crooms Academy through eighth grade and then went to Atlanta University to complete high school and teacher training. She became best friends with Beulah McDonald, who along with her husband, "Professor" Cartwright, took teaching jobs at the Hungerford Normal and

This was my mother's father, A.N. Johnson, as a young man.

Industrial School in Eatonville. My grandmother visited them there.

Having divorced her first husband in 1916, MaMa later married my grandfather, Augustus Newsome Johnson, an architect and builder. In 1922, he was hired to build a home for Hungerford's principal, Russell Calhoun. The Johnson family lived in Orlando for the first part of the 1920s and traveled to Eatonville to visit friends. Around 1925, A.N. Johnson moved his family to Lakeland, Florida, where he became a successful builder. He designed and built the First Baptist Church as well as Harmony Baptist Church. He also completed the two-story Palace Casino Dance Hall, now an Elks Lodge.

A.N. Johnson enjoyed America's prosperity, but when the Depression struck and he lost everything, he decided to move his family to Eatonville on the thirty-three acres of land he had bought during the 1920s.

Though my grandfather was an important part of my upbringing, the person who had the most sustained influence on me was my grandmother. She was strong-willed, and, I believe, made an effort to instill in me a particular way of seeing things. By the instructions she gave me, the expressions she used, the discussions we had, she groomed me to

For a time in the '30s, Zora lived in this house called Tuxedo Junction across the lake from my grandmother, Addie G. Johnson.

My mother, Ella Johnson Dinkins, enjoys the water. Here she is in her early 20s.

be self-confident.

It was MaMa who first introduced me to Zora Neale Hurston. Zora's stories were the same ones she would tell me at bedtime. I couldn't wait to be scared to death by Raw-Head-And-Bloody-Bones and The Boogey Man. Zora's sayings were an integral part of my grandmother's conversations. When I would ask too many "what if" questions, she'd reply, "If a bullfrog had wings, he wouldn't bump his head so hard." As I grew older, MaMa would explain how women had "the keys to the kitchen." She encouraged me to think for myself and take "no wooden nickels."

Though in some quarters of Eatonville Zora may have been a source of consternation, in our family she was a celebrity. During the late 1930s, she lived across the lake from my family at Tuxedo Junction. She visited with my grandmother and took an interest in her children, teaching my Uncle Sam to play bridge and seeking a swimming scholarship for my Uncle Gus at Rollins College.

Though I did not read any of Zora Neale Hurston's books until I was 25 and had given birth to my first child, her influence was like a thread running through my childhood. Along with W.E.B. DuBois, who had taught MaMa at Atlanta University, Zora was a reference point my grandmother used to indicate how far she thought I could go.

I encountered this same live-up-to-your-potential theme at St. Lawrence A.M.E. Church, Eatonville's oldest house of worship. In fact, the church was older than the town. The same families who had founded the church in 1882 were the spiritual heads of the church when I attended Sunday School in the 1950s.

I can still see Miss Matilda Moseley, the Sunday School Superintendent and grandniece of Eatonville's founder, Joe Clarke, standing at the front pew, on the left side of the old clapboard church, surrounded by huge paintings of angels, Jesus, and people, all painted a dark brown and with African features. She encouraged us children, five, six, and seven years of age, to be proud of ourselves and of Eatonville. "When I mail a letter," she said, "I write the return address as Eatonville, not Maitland. I'm proud that Eatonville is a Negro town and I want everyone to know where I come from."

At St. Lawrence, children were taught to be leaders. We stood and recited before our class; we read scripture as part of the worship service; we attended Sunday School conventions and made reports to the congregation about what had occurred. We were urged to go forward, to graduate from high school and to go on to college. Young people going away to school knew they could count on $25 from St. Lawrence to help with expenses.

This dedication to education was not peculiar to the congregation I grew up in; the institutionalization of learning was part-and-parcel of the community itself. Just as St. Lawrence and Macedonia Baptist churches were spiritual centers, so, too, The Hungerford Industrial School and Eatonville Elementary School were focal points for the families whose children attended them.

Courtesy of Ella Dinkins

Pictured here are my grandmother, Addie G. Johnson, my mother, Ella Johnson Dinkins, and I as a newborn outside my grandmother's home.

I grew up hearing about life at Hungerford, a private boarding school where students helped to raise their food and where Cap'n Hall, the principal, ruled with an iron hand. The Hungerford School was named in honor of Robert

Hungerford, a relative of local white philanthropists who donated money for the school. The school was patterned after Booker T. Washington's Tuskegee Institute in Alabama. In fact, Washington had dispatched from Tuskegee Russell Calhoun, his wife, Mary, and some other teachers to establish the school in Eatonville.

Hungerford graduates possessed the practical skills to earn a living — carpentry, animal husbandry, domestic arts, etc. — and the social graces to comfortably handle group settings.

Courtesy of Ella Dinkins

Hungerford graduates have retained their lessons. If you call the home of Mrs. Hoyt Fuller, a lady in her late eighties, and ask to speak to her, she responds in a fragile voice, "It is she speaking." Similarly, Mama, who is in her early seventies, is a stickler about time. She can be counted on to repeat Cap'n Hall's saying on this subject whenever she feels the situation warrants: "Start on time if there's only one person there."

This picture of me was taken in the mid '50s on our lakefront in Eatonville.

Hungerford represented a way of life. The school was a shared community experience and its society helped to bind even closer an already tight-knit community. For example, some of our dearest family friends come out of the Hungerford School. Cap'n Hall and his wife, Mother Hall, were friends of Granddad and MaMa; their daughters, Minnie Hall Fields and Vivian Hall Boston, were classmates and friends of my mother and my aunts; and my best childhood friend, Mary Cecelia Boston McClendon, is the daughter of Vivian Hall Boston: three generations of relationships. This same pattern repeats itself whether the families involved are the Franklins, the Joneses, the Millers, the Moseleys, the

Reeds or the Smiths.

Hungerford School was more, however, than a training ground for life. The school represented Eatonville's collective wisdom on priorities and how to provide for future generations.

The people of Eatonville knew that the Hungerford School was very important. Many of the town's adults had not had formal training, but, as a community, it was their intention that the town's children always get a good education. That is why, even after the institution's founding, they continued to donate land to the school.

This commitment to learning distinguishes the Eatonville community. At a time in the country's history when children worked and only went to school when the family didn't need their labor, when book learning was a luxury reserved for

Courtesy of Harriett Moseley

This is a group picture of St. Lawrence's Sunday School students. Mary Cecelia Boston McClendon, my best childhood friend, is on the first stair at the far left; I am at the far right, next to Hernandez Miller, the girl with the ribbon in her hair.

those who could afford it, Eatonville guaranteed its children an inheritance of education.

There were two schools in Eatonville. Students in grades eight through twelve attended the Hungerford School. Before my grandfather built the one-room Eatonville Elementary School in 1922, children in the lower grades attended classes at the Oddfellows Hall, a building that housed several of Eatonville's social and fraternal organizations. By the time I was ready for first grade in 1953, Eatonville's children could no longer go to school in the community; we were bused to the newly constructed Webster Elementary School in Winter Park (now known as the Winter Park Adult Vocational School), which was built for the African-American youngsters of that city and the surrounding areas to the west.

Though I didn't go to school in Eatonville, my teachers came from there and so the success of my education was doubly ensured because they and my family worked together to see me achieve.

As a child, I was high-strung. I sucked two fingers in public until I was in second grade, I was petrified of heights and scared to death of cracks in sidewalks. If not a certified "basket case," I know my family and teachers were nonetheless concerned that I conquer these problems.

Mrs. Williams, my second grade teacher, whose people came to Eatonville in 1893, helped me overcome two of my anxieties. Fingers doused liberally with hot sauce and wrapped tightly in gauze, which I dared not remove, proved the perfect remedy for finger sucking.

Mrs. Williams also helped me manage my fear of heights. During my four years at Webster, she was responsible for the children's extracurricular activities — Christmas pageants, school plays and the like. When I was in second and third grades, she chose me as the lead for our school plays. The only problem was I as queen had to ascend a throne. My job was to climb the stairs leading to a wide table on which sat a chair. I had to go up! When rehearsals began, I dreaded what should have been my greatest moment. I can still remember how my teacher and some of her helpers tried to coax and cajole me: "You can do it," they'd say. "Don't be afraid; we won't let you fall." And somehow, I would make it through my performances. At the play's end, I even allowed our principal,

Courtesy of Ella Dinkins

Two of Eatonville's 'grand old ladies,' (left) Miss Matilda Moseley and my grandmother, Addie G. Johnson. Both have since died.

Mrs. Davis, to bring me to the edge of the raised stage to take my bow.

While my teachers were helping me at school, my mother had to contend with me at home. I was truly irrational when we went "up town," what we called our trips to Orlando.

Mama never hesitated though to take me with her and my grandmother. She was calm and amazingly dignified for what she would endure. I was okay until I had to get out of the car and face the cracks in the sidewalk. I would beg not to proceed. Sobbing, I would cling to Mama's legs, pushing her skirt up. While she was pushing her skirt down and calming me, she also was answering questions from concerned passersby.

Recalling my early years, I wonder now how I could have moved past my fetish and my fears had not my teachers and my mother cared for me as they did. Not only Mrs. Williams, but Mrs. Staggers, Mrs. Price, Mrs. Jenkins all loved me and I knew it. I also knew they'd report me to my mother and I knew if the report weren't good, I'd get a "whipping" at home for the paddle in the hand I had gotten at school. My mother backed my teachers; my teachers reaffirmed my mother. With this kind of support system, how could I lose?

The summer after fourth grade, my brother Anthony and I

visited with my Aunt Mary and Uncle Billie in upstate New York. After much family discussion, it was decided that Anthony and I should attend school in Saratoga Springs for a year. What began as a one-year experiment lasted through my graduation from high school.

Though I went to school "up North," my identity with Eatonville remained strong. Upon my return each summer, I visited with community friends like Mr. Mack Robinson and his wife, Miss Mattie; Mr. Charley Reed and his wife, Miss Mary Jane; Miss Matilda Moseley and a host of others. They all saw my northern schooling as directly benefitting the town. "Eatonville could really be something," they'd say, "if young people like you would come back and help out."

Chief among the persons who kept before me my responsibility to the town was our longtime family friend, George G. Townsel. A man of keen intellect, high standards and unquestioned integrity, Mr. Townsel was a student of government and a patriot. He used to speak with great intensity about the U.S. Constitution and the Declaration of Independence. To him, the greatness of the United States rested in our participatory democracy, and for him, there were no limits to the promise of Eatonville. He continually reminded me of the town's heritage, and he was merciless in his criticism of those, inside or outside the town, who held Eatonville back. He spit out the words he used to condemn Orange County when he would say, "Every kind of vice and corruption is allowed to take place in Eatonville because the county

Courtesy of Margaret Coleman

Mr. George Townsel, one of the important influences in my life, was in his nineties when this picture was taken with his goddaughter's grandson, Paul Cody.

allows it to take place."

Mr. Townsel was a philosopher and he helped mold my thinking during my formative years. Visits with him required concentration; he was not lecturing but, by his manner,

These paintings of Eatonville's mayors serve to remind today's Hungerford Elementary students of the town's proud heritage.

commanded my involvement in the ideas he expressed.

I couldn't have asked for a better upbringing. I had the love of family and friends, the security of neighbors, the example of achievers from within my community and a community itself with historic beginnings.

As I've reflected on why Eatonville means so much to me, I think the answer lies in the relationships I formed from my earliest days. The strength of the Eatonville community, I

▼

believe, lies in those relationships — families, neighbors, friends — and in the sharing of a common heritage, striving toward goals of mutual benefit and cooperation. In this environment, an individual need feel no limitations.

As I've listened to others discuss Zora and the Eatonville community she has made special to millions, I know that the wonder of my experience is the fact that it was and still is typical for other residents of the town. For us, Eatonville has been like a cocoon. We have been prepared to compete in life outside the community because the community inside has allowed us to develop in an ideal environment.

Over these last three years, I have learned so much and I have matured a great deal. It is my prayer that my children and their children and those who follow them also will have the opportunity to know and to love the Eatonville community. It is for this reason that I and my colleagues work so hard to preserve this special part of America.

DISCOVERY

▼

My colleague John Hicks loved to write, perhaps as much as Zora Neale Hurston.

When John was on the staff of *Florida* magazine, and I its editor, he always took great care in selecting his next profile. And I watched from a close distance as his curiosity always seemed to clear several hurdles — admiration being the first. That usually turned into a fascination, then as the portrait would emerge, I could tell it had become an obsession of his to tell an untold story.

I'll remember him as one of the finest writers to pass through *The Orlando Sentinel*. He could write about race car drivers and poets with equal grace. His energetic and intelligent approach to research never lapsed. That frustrated some of his editors who literally had to stand over him and seize his manuscripts from his typewriter. John would polish his stories forever if you let him.

He was witty and wise beyond his years. Unlike some of his crustier colleagues who with time had developed a hardening of the soul, John was a gentle spirit who cared so much about his subjects, both before and after his stories were published.

John died from a brain tumor in 1989, but his words on Eatonville's black author have taken on a life of their own.

His Sunday supplement story about Zora was nothing short of a magazine masterpiece. It was one article I just couldn't cut. We devoted an entire issue of *Florida* magazine to it and shortly afterward published it as a keepsake in booklet form. In January 1990, the *Sentinel* condensed it in the Style section to commemorate the 1st Annual Zora Neale Hurston Festival in Eatonville. John's story appears here in its entirety.

If *The Orlando Sentinel* deserves any credit for this tribute to Zora Neale Hurston, then we graciously accept and take our bows in John's behalf . . . remembering, of course, that the real inspiration that pricked his journalistic interest was the charming storyteller herself.

— Bill Dunn
Managing Editor of *The Orlando Sentinel*

*Died: Zora Neale Hurston, 57, Florida-born Negro author who explored the world of Negro folklore and magic in remote parts of the South and the West Indies, celebrated the big trials and small triumphs of the Southern Negro in a series of novels (**Jonah's Gourd Vine, Seraph on the Suwanee**) without succumbing to bitterness; in Fort Pierce, Fla.—**Time** magazine, Feb. 15, 1960.*

by John Hicks

In Fort Pierce, the nodding, yellow-flowered weeds grow wild over the grave of Zora Neale Hurston, concealing, then revealing the small, gray stone that proclaims to a blind-deaf day that the dust of greatness is hidden here:

ZORA NEALE HURSTON
"A GENIUS OF THE SOUTH"
1901 — 1960
NOVELIST, FOLKLORIST
ANTHROPOLOGIST

Unseen insects zzzt underfoot, and sandspurs leap onto the clothing of the visitor. Trash and junk litter The Garden of the Heavenly Rest, as it is called, this abandoned graveyard at the dead-end of North 17th Street.

Within the vine-covered, fading pink, concrete entrance gate of the graveyard, a group of black children bat a baseball. They glance from the corners of their eyes at the stranger who contemplates the grave.

Who, they wonder, WAS this Zora Neale Hurston whose grave draws perhaps 100 pilgrims a year to a weed lot tucked into a far corner of black Fort Pierce?

Who, the stranger wonders, IS Zora Neale Hurston, this living spirit who has cast her spell on him, webbing him to her, tugging him into the sweltering heat of an uncertain quest?

It is a question not easily answered.

"Nothing that God ever made is the same thing to more

than one person. That is natural. There is no single face in nature, because every eye that looks upon it, sees it from its own angle." — Zora Neale Hurston, in her autobiography, *Dust Tracks on a Road.*

"Zora Neale Hurston is a literary artist of sufficient talent to deserve intensive study, both as an artist and as an intellect. She deserves an important place in American literary history." — Dr. Robert Hemenway, *Zora Neale Hurston, A Literary Biography*, University of Illinois Press, 1977.

"She was very bold and outspoken — an attractive woman who had learned how to survive with native wit. She approached life as a series of encounters and challenges; most of these she overcame without succumbing to the maudlin bitterness of many of her contemporaries."
— Larry Neal, the introduction to *Dust Tracks on a Road*, J.B. Lippincott Co., 1971 .

"Because of her simple style, humor, and folklore, Zora Neale Hurston deserves more recognition than she ever earned. But, superficial and shallow in her artistic and social judgments, she became neither an impeccable raconteur nor a scholar. Always, she remained a wandering minstrel."
— Dr. Darwin T. Turner, *In a Minor Chord, Three Afro-American Writers and Their Search for Identity*, Southern Illinois University Press, 1971.

"She was a liberated woman who was ahead of her time. She described it as it was in those books." — Mrs. Anne Key, librarian at the Zora Neale Hurston Library in Eatonville, Zora's birthplace.

"She had style and was flamboyant in an intellectual way."
— Marjorie Silver Alder, Fort Pierce, a former St. Lucie County commissioner, a radio and newspaper journalist, perhaps Zora Hurston's closest friend in her final few years of life.

"The information she expounded held people — you couldn't see Zora for what she was saying." — Dr. Clem C. Benton, Fort Pierce, physician and friend of Zora.

"She wasn't that popular around here because she tried to write about local people, and they resented the way she tried to picture them." — Mrs. Geraldine Otey, retired teacher, Eatonville resident, acquaintance of Zora.

"She was a loner. She was friendly and casual, but at the close of the day, she went her way and the world went its way." — C.E. Bolen, editor of the *Fort Pierce Chronicle*, a black newspaper where Zora was employed briefly near the end of her life.

It is not far on the Florida map from the dirt backroads of Fort Pierce to those of Eatonville, the small black city near Orlando where Zora Hurston first opened her eyes on a world of wonder; but for those who seek Zora's wandering spirit, the road between is long, sinuous, dappled with mysterious shadows.

Zora Neale Hurston: anthropologist; folklorist; novelist; impassioned poet-hoodoo priestess of the black South; the flamboyant "Princess Zora," companion to novelist Fannie Hurst; contributor to the 1920s Harlem Negro Renaissance in arts and literature; drama instructor; playwright; singer; dancer — and, at times, cook, housemaid, manicurist, waitress.

This portrait of young Zora showed her to be a striking woman.

The bright images of Zora Hurston, or "Zora Neale," as friends, black and white, often affectionately call her, leap and laugh in the senses; the dim ones merely befuddle with seeming incongruity.

She is an enigma, this accomplished black woman who, fired by her mother's exhortation to "jump at de sun," hurdled barriers of race, sex, poverty and obscurity to sail, seemingly, to an even brighter star, but then plummeted and was extinguished—in poverty and obscurity.

An untethered spirit, she glided on wings of imagination

and wanderlust throughout the United States and the West Indies, gathering in life, transforming it into living words of color and rhythm.

Like the character Janie in her novel *Their Eyes Were Watching God*, Zora Neale "pulled in her horizon like a great fish-net. Pulled it from around the waist of the world and draped it over her shoulder. So much of life in its meshes! She called in her soul to come and see."

She took what she had gathered, electrified it with the thunder and lightning poetry bequeathed to her by her father, John, an irrepressible Baptist preacher, set it to her own, African-drumming heartbeat and gave us . . .

. . . books of magic and folklore, *Mules and Men*, 1935; *Tell My Horse*, 1938; novels, *Jonah's Gourd Vine*, 1934; *Their Eyes Were Watching God*, 1937; *Moses, Man of the Mountain*, 1939; *Seraph on the Suwanee*, 1948; an autobiography, *Dust Tracks on a Road*, 1942; short stories, plays, music, songs, multitudinous newspaper and magazine articles.

She was a celebration of black life, and all life. She drew from the deep well of black Africa the spirit that nourished the roots of black America and sustained "Cuffy," the black human enslaved by the white "bukra."

"So they danced," she wrote in *Jonah's Gourd Vine*. "They called for the instrument that they had brought to America in their skins — the drum — and they played upon it . . . It was said, 'He will serve us better if we bring him from Africa naked and thingless.' So the bukra reasoned. They tore away his clothes that Cuffy might bring nothing away, but Cuffy seized his drum and hid it in his skin under the skull bones."

But, by the time of her death, Jan. 28, 1960, in a segregated Fort Pierce nursing home, the exuberant songs had ceased. She was penniless, virtually forgotten.

Newspaper articles announcing her decline and death stirred old memories. Donations from friends, publishers, the community paid the undertaker. She was returned to the Florida dust in the Garden of the Heavenly Rest and, again, virtually forgotten.

But why, the stranger at her grave wonders, did she come here to Fort Pierce, out of the bright lights, into oblivion, to die and be buried? Why?

"The strangest thing about it was that once I found the use of my feet, they took to wandering. I always wanted to go. I would wander off in the woods all alone, following some inside urge to go places. This alarmed my mother a great deal. She used to say that she believed a woman who was an enemy of hers had sprinkled 'travel dust' around the doorstep the day I was born." — *Dust Tracks on a Road.*

"From 1912 until her death in 1960, Zora Neale Hurston wandered, rarely remaining in one locality for longer than three years and often disappearing from public view despite her prominence as the author of four novels, two collections of tales, and an autobiography — more books than any other female Afro-American had written" — Darwin T. Turner, *In a Minor Chord.*

"She moved every time you turned, and she'd been everywhere." — Mrs. Mabel (Clifford J.) Hurston, Sanford, widow of Zora's brother.

According to her own account, Zora Neale took her first steps on the road that eventually led her to Fort Pierce at the age of nine, following her mother's death, an account subject to some doubt because Zora was often vague about her age. "That hour began my wanderings," she wrote in *Dust Tracks.* "Not so much in geography, but in time. Then not so much in time as spirit."

The seventh* of eight children — six boys, two girls — she meandered from relative to relative, began taking menial jobs at the age of 14 to support herself, and, at 15, ran away from a brother's home to work as a maid to an actress with a Gilbert and Sullivan repertoire company.

This employment carried her North, to Baltimore, where the actress married, terminating Zora's employment and forcing her, she wrote, "to take up my pilgrim's stick and go outside again."

Taking a waitress job to support herself, she entered night school. There, she found her calling, inspired by an English teacher's vivid rendition of Coleridge's poem *Kubla Khan.*

This impressive interpretation, she recalled in *Dust Tracks,* had allowed her to visualize "all that the writer had meant for me to see with him, and infinite cosmic things besides."

* Family records show that she was the fifth of eight children.

Zora was an enthusiastic convert. "This was my world, I said to myself, and I shall be in it and surrounded by it, if it is the last thing I do on God's green dirt-ball," she wrote in her autobiography.

It was a vow she upheld throughout the rest of her life, though it exacted an often cruel price in severed relationships, disillusionment, privation and ill health.

She was graduated from the high school division of Morgan College in Baltimore in 1918 and entered Howard University in Washington.

There, her writing ability began to manifest itself in 1921 when, as a member of the Howard literary club, the Stylus, she published her first short story, *John Redding Goes to Sea*, in the club's magazine.

Acquiring an education was not easy, or free, and Zora worked, at times, as a manicurist, maid and waitress in a struggle to keep ahead of her debts while at Howard.

Then, in her sophomore year, she was awarded a scholarship to attend Barnard College in New York City as the school's first black student. She received a bachelor of arts degree from Barnard in 1928.

But, more importantly, she had arrived in the big city smack in the middle of the Harlem Renaissance, an effulgent spinoff of the Jazz Age when white liberals encouraged and promoted black writers and artists, at times, to the point of a fad.

Zora, as bold and brassy as the era, quickly fell in with the accomplished crowd, the country girl from Florida

Courtesy of Robert Hemenway

Zora while a student at Howard University, c. 1919-23

finding herself in the company of such literary greats as Langston Hughes, Wallace Thurman, Arna Bontemps.

Zora's 1920s experience was heady stuff for a young college girl, but she maintained her balance and her output, producing the short stories *Drenched in Light*, *Spunk and Sweat* and the play *Color Struck*, among other offerings of the decade.

Her burgeoning ability also had brought Zora to the attention of popular novelist Fannie Hurst who hired her as a secretary in 1925. When Zora proved hopelessly inept, Miss Hurst fired her — but allowed her to stay on for more than a year as companion and chauffeur.

It was during a trip to Vermont that Fannie Hurst conferred the title of African royalty, "Princess," on Zora in order to integrate a restaurant.

Despite some critics' views that Zora was totally oblivious to racial inequities, personal or otherwise, and deliberately ignored the suffering of her own people, this episode went down hard.

Miss Hurst later wrote that, when Zora had finished the meal, she said, "Who would think that a good meal could be so bitter."

The timing of Miss Hurst's pronouncement may have been wrong, but the title was apt. Zora had the imposing aura of a princess. She was well-suited to her calling and to the Roaring Twenties.

In an autobiographical sketch in *Twentieth Century Authors*, Zora later would describe the young Zora as "a bright pupil, but impudent," winsome traits she artfully employed to gain favor and financial aid, primarily from white people, to assist her in her studies.

But there was more to Zora Hurston than just brashness and scheming. Even late in life when the fire was burning low, people would be drawn by an extraordinarily compelling quality, a physical presence and spiritual magnetism.

Though she caricatured herself as having a "face looking like it had been chopped out of a knot of pine wood with a hatchet on somebody's off day," her photographs reveal a woman of strong character, penetrating gaze and earthy beauty.

Tall, at five-six, attired in stylish, often exotic clothing, her sloe eyes laughing and playing, young Zora must have been irresistible, and it is easy to understand why people would be drawn to her and eager to help her.

Zora seemed blind to the color of her patrons. She had experienced no racial trauma in all-black, self-governing Eatonville, and she professed not to be concerned with race.

"I am not tragically colored," she wrote in a 1928 magazine article. "There is no great sorrow dammed up in my soul, nor lurking behind my eyes."

In *Dust Tracks*, she would state that she had "no race prejudice of any kind." But hers was a peculiar, sometimes precarious position. She shuttled to and fro between the races, carrying the riches of black culture to a white market and hovering about the borderline of the races.

At times, she seemed to one side or the other of that line and, at other times, stuck right on the border.

And, to compound this ambivalence, the manner of her ascension had attracted the lightning of some black critics. Langston Hughes, famed black poet and author, wrote of Zora in an oft-quoted passage from his 1940 autobiography, *The Big Sea:*

"In her youth she was always getting scholarships and things from wealthy white people, some of whom simply paid her just to sit around and represent the Negro race for them, she did it in such a racy fashion . . . To many of her white friends, no doubt, she was a perfect 'darkie,' in the nice meaning they give the term — that is a naive, childlike, sweet, humorous and highly colored Negro."

But Hughes also admitted that Zora was "a student who didn't let college give her a broad A and who had great scorn for all pretensions, academic or otherwise. That is why she was such a fine folklore collector, able to go among the people and never act as if she had been to school at all."

Hughes, who also had received the benefits of white patronage during the 1920s, may have had more than race pride in mind when he wrote that mixed opinion of Zora.

Dr. Robert Hemenway in his scholarly, detailed and revealing *Zora Neale Hurston, A Literary Biography*, points out Hughes and Zora had quarreled bitterly over a collaborative effort, the play, *Mule Bone: A Comedy of Negro Life*, in 1931.

The play was never produced because of the wrangling,

and the quarrel killed a fast friendship between the two artists.

Even in 1954, Zora still was bitter on the subject of Langston Hughes. In a business letter to the *Saturday Evening Post*, a copy of which is in the possession of Marjorie Alder, she wrote of him:

"I thought him very innocent-like and full of simplicity and virtues. I was to discover later that his shy-looking mien covered a sly opportunism that was utterly revolting."

In words that underlined the unusual, sometimes contradictory, conservatism she often expressed in her later years, she added, "I found out about communists from him."

But all this was far distant as Zora completed her education and prepared to conquer "God's green dirt-ball."

If visions of *Kubla Khan* had unlatched the gate to her future road, her study of anthropology under renowned Dr. Franz Boas at Columbia University in the late 1920s threw the gate wide.

It was Boas, her "Papa Franz," as she playfully called him, who arranged a fellowship that enabled Zora, in February 1927, to go home from college to Florida, to Eatonville, to collect the folklore of her people.

Zora had begun to "jump at de sun." She

Courtesy of Harriett Moseley

Joe Clarke's Store. The social center of Eatonville, men and women gathered here to swap stories and "tell lies".

had taken the first of many long-strided steps on that twisting, dusty road.

"I hurried back to Eatonville because I knew that the town was full of material and that I could get it without hurt, harm or danger. As early as I could remember it was the habit of the men folks particularly to gather on the store porch of evenings and swap stories. Even the women folks would stop and break a breath with them at times . . .

So I rounded Park Lake and came speeding down the straight stretch into Eatonville, the city of five lakes, three croquet courts, three hundred brown skins, three hundred good swimmers, plenty guavas, two schools and no jailhouse" — Zora Hurston, *Mules and Men.*

Mules and Men has been described by famed folklorist Alan Lomax as "the best single book on Negro folklore in the U.S."

But Zora, characteristically, did not arrive at this renown directly. As she admits in *Dust Tracks*, her first six months of folklore collecting were "disappointing" because "the glamor of Barnard College was still upon me."

She returned to New York "with my heart beneath my knees and my knees in some lonesome valley," and "stood before Papa Franz and cried salty tears."

Boas gave her "a good going over," she wrote. "He knew I was green and feeling my oats and that only bitter disappointment was going to purge me. It did."

Zora overcame her initial failure in grand style when she returned to the field under the sponsorship of Mrs. Rufus Osgood Mason, a wealthy patron of the Afro-American arts, in December 1927.

Mrs. Mason contributed approximately $15,000 to Zora's work during the following five years, Hemenway writes, aid that helped Zora become the foremost black folklore collector of the day.

But, though Zora admits her initial failure, she does not admit that it drove her to, in Hemenway's words, "that most grievous of academic sins — plagiarizing the work of another."

An essay Zora wrote about Cudjo Lewis, the sole survivor of what is believed to have been the last slave ship to

America in 1859, was, Hemenway writes in his biography of Zora, "25 per cent original research and the rest shameless plagiarism from a book entitled *Historic Sketches of the Old South.*"

The book, by Emma Langdon Roche, had been published 13 years before Zora's essay. Linguist William Stewart first discovered the plagiarism in 1972, and Hemenway's account of it is, he states, "the first public discussion of Stewart's discovery."

Zora evaded professional disaster only because her theft was not discovered, and, according to Hemenway, "She never plagiarized again; she became a major folklore collector."

But, whatever her sins, Zora continued along her dusty road, pausing in Eau Gallie, now part of Melbourne, Fla., in 1929, to write the mountain of fascinating material that would make up *Mules and Men*, and then moving on.

In *Mules and Men*, Zora recorded not only the tall tales and 1920s lifestyles of some Eatonville residents and other black Floridians, but the rough life in the "jooks" of Polk County, where she nearly was knifed in a barroom brawl, and her eerie experiences in New Orleans where she became a hoodoo "doctor" to better understand the subject.

Mules and Men is packed with stories bearing such flavorful titles as "How the Woodpecker Nearly Drowned the Whole World" and "Why the Porpoise Has His Tail on Crossways."

But one of the most memorable and colorfully delivered anecdotes is "Why Women Always Take Advantage of Men," told by Eatonville resident Matilda Moseley.

Essentially, the story details the early days of man and woman on earth, when their strength was equal. Man, frustrated by his inability to "whip" woman persuades God to give him more strength so he can "make her mind."

Woman, unable to get God to grant her strength equal to man's, is advised by the devil to obtain from God "dat bunch of keys hangin' by de mantelpiece." She does, and the devil advises her she can now lock man out of the kitchen and the bedroom and away from the cradle, or "his generations."

Denied access to these three essential areas, man has to submit to the woman.

The tale reaches poetic heights in the man's plea for more

strength from "Ole Maker, wid de mawnin' stars glitterin' in yo' shinin' crown, wid de dust from yo' footsteps makin' worlds upon worlds, wid de blazin' bird we call de sun flyin' out of yo' right hand in de mawnin' . . ."

It depicts man and woman nearly on equal footing with God, wide awake to nature and integral, if small, parts of the cosmos . . . themes Zora Hurston would express again and again.

A wonderful thing about this story, also, is that its teller Matilda Moseley is still alive, residing on a dust-drifted side road in Eatonville.

She is a slender, white-haired, light-tan woman. She is 87 now, and her memory falters so that she is like a delicate autumn leaf fluttering in the wind of time, speckles of brilliant sunlight occasionally beaming through her, past tangled branches.

But she remembers Zora Neale, and she tells you, with a full-throated laugh, "We were regular, little old buddies. We got our education at practically the same time. She went away, and I stayed at home and had a few little chickens." And she laughs again.

Courtesy of Harriett Moseley.

A 1960's picture of Matilda Moseley. (to her left) her daughter Mildred Grant; her great grandson, Reginald Moseley; her granddaughter, Harriett Moseley. Descendants of Joe Clarke, founder of Eatonville.

"We lived in a big two-story house over there," she says, pointing down the dusty lane toward Kennedy Avenue, the main street of Eatonville, "and she lived in a two-story house back up this way. I would be upstairs, and she would holler — I could hear her holler." Again, her young laugh as she recalls two little girls long ago.

Memory weaves in and about the branches. Mrs. Moseley looks to her daughter, Mrs. Mildred Grant, sitting nearby. "I dreamed about Zora night before last," she whispers, glancing back over the long, dusty road she has journeyed.

Other people in Eatonville do not remember Zora Neale so fondly. Her books frequently dealt with the raw and unvarnished aspects of black life, and those whose names and town she used did not always take kindly to it.

Still, Zora Neale returned often over the years, staying with Eatonville folks, then drifting on, the dust from her footsteps "makin' worlds upon worlds" of fact and fancy.

"Zora gets so much of the black experience. Boy, the things she said, her degree of authenticity. She came closer to representing what was on the hearts and minds of the people, as far as black people are concerned, than her critics." — Dr. Alzo Reddick, director of placement, Rollins College, Winter Park, Florida, a student of Zora Hurston's writing.

Mules and Men, although written earlier than *Jonah's Gourd Vine*, did not appear in print until after the novel was published in 1934.

Zora wrote in *Dust Tracks* that the Great Depression dried up research funds and, consequently, in May 1932, she found herself in Eatonville with a "huge mass of material" that, edited and set aside, later would become *Mules and Men*.

Hemenway writes that the money actually continued coming from Mrs. Mason until the fall of 1932, but such inconsistencies routinely pop up in an investigation of the life of Zora Hurston.

The Story of Zora Neale Hurston, Author, a biographical sketch by Dr. Edwin Osgood Grover, professor of books at Rollins College, from 1926 to 1951, tells us that Zora went into a Winter Park bookstore in the spring of 1932 and inquired how one went about getting a book published.

She was referred to Grover who had 30 years experience in publishing, and he and other members of the Rollins faculty assisted Zora, both in her writing endeavors and in the presentation of two folk concerts, *From Sun to Sun*, performed at Rollins Feb. 11, 1933, and *All De Live Long Day*, presented Jan. 5, 1934.

It was in these representations of black "folk life" that Zora displayed her talents, not only as a writer and director but as a singer and dancer, according to copies of printed programs for the two concerts filed in the Rollins archives.

The Rollins concerts also reflected Zora's presentation of *The Great Day* at the John Golden Theater in New York City, Jan. 10, 1932, a program Hemenway terms "an unqualified success."

Additionally, in commenting on strict anti-commercial restraints Mrs. Mason placed on the fruits of Zora's collecting, thus preventing more widespread and entertaining distribution of the material, Hemenway writes:

"A stage version of *Mules and Men* might have had the same impact as the televising of Alex Haley's *Roots*."

Though the sketch by Dr. Grover, who died in 1965, sheds light on Zora's work, it also contributes to the mystery of her life. Grover wrote that Zora "was born in a small Georgia town, but her family moved to Eatonville, Florida, when she was just a child."

Clearing up this mystery is as difficult as clearing up other discrepancies in the life of Zora Hurston. There is no birth certificate for her on file in the Florida Bureau of Vital Statistics in Jacksonville, and the state of Georgia does not maintain a central file of birth certificates for the years before 1919.

But, when dealing with the life of Zora Hurston, one quickly learns never to deny the possibility of anything.

Creative juices flowing, Zora wrote *The Gilded Six Bits*, one of her best short stories, in early 1933 and gave it to Rollins professor Robert Wunsch to read. Wunsch, in turn, read it to his writing class, then mailed it to *Story* magazine.

The story, published in the August 1933 issue of *Story*, attracted the attention of the J.B. Lippincott publishing company which sent Zora a letter, asking if she were, by any chance, writing a novel.

She apparently wasn't, but she informed Lippincott she was, quickly rented a small house in Sanford, Florida, for $1.50 a week and hammered out *Jonah's Gourd Vine* "in about three months," according to *Dust Tracks.*

She borrowed $2 to cover the $1.83 postage to send the manuscript to the Lippincott Co., which telegraphed acceptance of the novel within two weeks, on Oct. 16, 1933, the same day Zora was evicted from her little house for nonpayment of $18 rent.

It was a precarious, hand-to-mouth existence, often repeated in many places.

Jonah's Gourd Vine also had grown out of Zora's Florida experiences. The novel was based on the life of her father, a spellbinding minister with a weakness for women. Again, from her black experience, she had drawn a powerful poetry, realized in such sermonic passages as:

"De Sun, Ah!
Gethered up de fiery skirts of her garments
And wheeled about de throne, Ah!
Saying, Ah, make man after me, ha!
God gazed upon the sun
And sent her back to her blood-red socket
And shook His head, ha!
De Moon, ha!
Grabbed up de reins of de tides.
And dragged a thousand seas behind her
As she walked around de throne
Ah-h, please make man after me
But God said "NO"!
De stars bust out from their diamond sockets
And circled de glitterin' throne cryin'
A-aah! Make man after me
God said, "NO"!
I'll make man in my own image, ha!"

Still tapping her heritage and experience, she next created *Their Eyes Were Watching God*, an unusual, touching story written, Zora noted in *Dust Tracks*, "to embalm all the tenderness of my passion" for a man she had loved.

She wrote this novel in Haiti in only seven weeks while researching voodoo under a Guggenheim fellowship. This and similar research in Jamaica resulted in *Tell My Horse*, a study of voodoo and lifestyles on the two West Indian islands in the late 1930s. *Tell My Horse* received mixed reviews and is, Hemenway states, "Hurston's poorest book."

Moses, Man of the Mountain, which retells the story of Moses from a black viewpoint, is Miss Hurston's "most accomplished achievement in fiction," according to Darwin

Turner. Hemenway terms *Moses* and *Their Eyes Were Watching God* Zora's "two masterpieces of the late thirties."

In *Moses*, the title character is a hoodoo practitioner who uses his awesome powers to make ole Pharaoh let the Israelites go. The novel not only views the legend-making process from a black perspective, but also challenges the traditional conception of Moses, the law-giver. It is replete with humor and such idiomatic gems as:

"Aaron tired to back off but Moses had him by his whiskers and wouldn't let him go. So Aaron cringed and fawned and said, 'Lord, Moses, you're my bossman, and I know it. I wouldn't think of putting myself on an equal with you. You're a great big high cockadoo and I ain't nothing. You done been round these people long enough to know 'em. You know they ain't nothing and if you and God fool with 'em you won't be nothing neither.' "

The autobiographical

Zora in her Chevy. She traveled by car when collecting folklore in the U.S.

Dust Tracks earned its author the *Saturday Review's* $1,000 Anisfield-Wolf Award for helping to improve race relations, but left some large gaps in the Zora Hurston story.

The book, for example, barely mentions Zora's first marriage and does not mention a second marriage at all. Hemenway, in *Zora Neale Hurston, A Literary Biography*, writes that she was married to Herbert Sheen from 1927 to 1931 and to Albert Price III from 1939 to 1943.

The legal lengths of the two marriages is deceptive because both, in reality, lasted only months. Zora's parting with Sheen was amicable, Hemenway writes — but adds that court records show Price accused Zora of threatening him with her voodoo powers during spats, which, as Hemenway notes, sounds "plausible."

Zora's marriages were doomed to failure because she already was married — to her work and her wandering. It was part of the price exacted by "the force from somewhere in Space which commands you to write in the first place," in Zora's words.

She completed *Dust Tracks* while employed as a story consultant at Paramount Studios in California. This seems no more incongruous than many other episodes in her life, particularly when one discovers she was in Hollywood only about three months in late 1941 and early 1942 and collecting folklore the following summer in her beloved Florida.

Dust Tracks is alternately poetic and annoying. Its deletions and vague chronology suggest Zora had much to hide, and there are passages where she sounds more like a Barnard sophomore than a sophisticated woman of the world.

But, as Hemenway points out, Zora was uncertain "what her editors and white audience expected" and some rather caustic commentary was excised from the manuscript of *Dust Tracks* before it was published. Hemenway includes some of the unused material in his book.

Those who, in Hughes' words, might have considered Zora the "perfect 'darkie'" probably would have been vastly upset to read that it "would be a good thing for the Anglo-Saxon to get the idea out of his head that everybody owes him something just for being blond. I am forced to the conclusion that two thirds of them do hold that view. The idea of human slavery is so deeply ground in that the pink-toes can't get it out of their system."

Dust Tracks became something of a critical success, though less of an autobiography and statement than it might have been. Zora made a little money, but at the cost of sounding at times like that "perfect 'darkie'" she must have despised.

Still, there is great beauty in *Dust Tracks*, brilliance in the midst of failing light.

Zora now found herself in demand as a black spokeswoman and magazine essayist, but her mighty fiction quill lay virtually unused.

For a painfully long six years, Zora did not publish a book. A proposed novel was rejected by Lippincott in 1945. And when *Seraph on the Suwanee* was released by her new publisher, Charles Scribner's Sons, in 1948, it was quite a departure from Zora's earlier works.

Though the characters in *Seraph* are recognizable as Hurston creations, the book concerns poor whites primarily, rather than blacks, has liberal amounts of sensation and sex and is heavy and, at times, depressing going, though well-written.

Seraph did not sell particularly well, and Zora Neale Hurston never had another book published, although she had articles accepted by magazines and newspapers.

But so what? Zora was rich, wasn't she? A persistent myth in the Zora Hurston saga is that she made enormous amounts of money from her books.

Hemenway writes, however, "She was published mostly during the Great Depression, and the largest royalty any of her books ever earned was $943.75 . . ."

Joseph Gillen, present-day treasurer of the Lippincott Co., which published Zora's first six books, said, when contacted in Philadelphia, that the firm's records show Zora made only about $500 each in royalties from *Mules and Men* and *Jonah's Gourd Vine* in the first five years they were sold.

Thus, even at the height of her career, Zora was usually toeing the ragged edge of financial disaster. Advances on her books, fellowships, occasional story and article sales, employment hither and yon, a couple of Works Progress Administration jobs and patronage evidently kept her in business during her most productive years, the hard years of the 1930s.

In and about her final major works, she continued her eccentric lifestyle, living on board a houseboat in Daytona Beach from 1943 to 1945 when she reportedly sold the vessel to help finance a search for a lost Mayan city in Honduras, a dubious and unsuccessful pursuit that occupied her fancy off and on into 1948.

Zora told people she also sold the rights to her books to help finance her Central America explorations, though Hemenway and other biographers offer no evidence to support this. Bradenton, Florida, writer Marian Murray, in a biographical sketch, stated Zora went broke when an improbable-sounding scheme to establish a black colony in Honduras failed.

In any event, Zora's star was clearly on the wane. In September 1948, just prior to the publication of *Seraph on the Suwanee*, Zora was arrested in New York City and subsequently indicted on a morals charge.

A 10-year-old boy accused Zora and two other adults of sodomy, according to Hemenway. Eventually, the indictment was dismissed, but the damage had been done.

Writer Larry Neal, in his introduction to the 1971 edition of *Dust Tracks*, wrote:

"All the evidence indicates that the charge was false since Zora was out of the country at the time of the alleged crime; but several of the Negro newspapers exploded it into a major scandal. Naturally, Zora was hurt, and the incident plunged her into a state of abject despair . . .

"There was no trial. The charges were dropped. But Zora Neale Hurston ceased to be a creative writer, although in the early fifties she had articles accepted by the *Saturday Evening Post* and the conservative *American Legion Magazine*."

Wings of fancy drooping, she continued her fall into anonymity. In 1950, James Lyons, a *Miami Herald* reporter, found Zora employed as a maid in a home on Rivo Alto Island.

Zora told him she was temporarily "written out" but that a novel and three short stories were in the hands of her agent. She was working as a domestic, she said, to "shift gears."

She also told Lyons she had tentative plans to start a national magazine by and for domestics, and she later would tell Marjorie Alder she had worked as a maid merely to gather material for an article.

"She was down on her luck. She had even pawned her typewriter and was living with some Puerto Ricans. I believe she had been headed for Honduras. But an Englishman and another man were managing her money, she said. The Englishman, I believe, took the money to the race track to make a killing and lost it all." — Mrs. Kenneth Burritt, Zora's employer on Rivo Alto Island.

Zora soon left her job as a maid and wandered north through Florida, returning in 1951 to the little house in Eau Gallie where she had compiled *Mules and Men* 22 years earlier. She was to remain there until 1956 when her landlord sold the property.

"In many ways," Hemenway writes, "it was the most peaceful period in a turbulent life." Zora barely existed on a thin trickle of income, but she enjoyed the pleasant surroundings near the bank of the Indian River.

In 1952, Zora resurfaced, this time as a reporter, covering the sensational Ruby McCollum murder trial in Live Oak, Fla., for the black newspaper, *The Pittsburgh Courier.*

Zora was incensed when an all-white jury convicted Mrs. McCollum, a black, and sentenced her to die for the killing of Dr. C. Leroy Adams, a state senate nominee.

In addition to reporting the trial, Zora brought author William Bradford Huie into the case and helped save Mrs. McCollum from death.

In 1956, Huie published a bestselling book, *Ruby McCollum: Woman in the Suwanee Jail,* with a chapter on the trial written by Zora.

This last hurrah of sorts behind her, Zora went back to struggling for existence in Eau Gallie.

She gave pep talks to students at the segregated Stone High School in Melbourne, exhorting them, as her mother had exhorted her, to strive to better themselves.

Pushed out of her nest in Eau Gallie, she wandered still farther north, to Cocoa, and east, to Merritt Island.

She took a job as a $1.85 an hour librarian in the Pan American technical library at Patrick Air Force Base near

Cocoa Beach from June, 1956, until May, 1957, when she was fired.

The official reason given was that Zora was "too well-educated for the job," Hemenway writes, but he also notes that Zora did not get along with her fellow employees and supervisor, a problem she seemed to encounter whenever she took a routine job.

But, still, despite everything, she continued to write wherever she went, pounding away at her typewriter, struggling to create, reaching for lost glory.

"She lived on what was then Fifth Street between Avocado and Guava in a very small house that has since been torn down. I missed her, and I didn't know why she left. I heard she was in Fort Pierce." — Mrs. Daisy Tucker, Melbourne, one-time friend of Zora Hurston.

"We went to the drive-in movie. They had a 'whites only' rest room. Zora said she was going to the rest room. I said, 'You can't; that's for whites only.' She said, 'I'm going,' and she did go." — J.N. Tucker, husband of Daisy Tucker.

"She didn't integrate the rest room; she commandeered it!" — Marjorie Alder, upon being told the preceding story.

"It was surprising to find her here and to find out how famous she was. She was quiet and unassuming about it all. I asked, 'Why didn't you let us know you were here?' She said,

October 1990 photograph of Zora's Fort Pierce home, 1734 Benton Quarters.

Photograph by N.Y. Nathiri

Site of Bolen's Fort Pierce Chronicle, *the African-American weekly for which Zora wrote.*

'Oh, I knew you'd find out soon enough.'" — Mrs. Flossie B. Bryant, Melbourne, retired Stone High School teacher.

"She lived here three years or more in an upstairs apartment. She did a lot of writing and typing. She didn't say what she was working on. She went about what she did, to herself, in a quiet way. I never read her books. I understand a lot of other people read them." — Mrs. Daisy Stone, Cocoa, who rented an apartment to Zora Hurston.

"We rescued her — she was almost out and gone. She was cast out on Merritt Island. I made a special trip up there to talk to her. I don't think she was working. She was planning on writing a book, but she never did get it into print." — C.E. Bolen.

Thus, Zora Neale Hurston's long, dusty, winding road had delivered her to Fort Pierce. It was the autumn of 1957.

She remained at Bolen's little weekly newspaper only "months," writing "some very good articles about the Indian River area and a column on magic," recollects the bespectacled Bolen, a tall, plump, dark-skinned man with a fringe of gray hair.

But she was frustrated. "She was a person who'd never had a boss," said Bolen. "She was a writer and, naturally, was pretty well set in her ways. That would cause some opposition, but we got along okay."

Zora soon quit to take a job as a substitute high school teacher at the all-black Lincoln Park Academy, on North 17th Street. There, as at Patrick AFB, she encountered problems and was quickly fired. The difficulties centered on a state teaching certificate, but Zora believed there was more to it than that.

"My name as an author is too big to be tolerated, lest it gather to itself the 'glory' of the school here. I have met that before. But perhaps it is natural. The mediocre have no importance except through appointment. They feel invaded and defeated by the presence of creative folk among them." — Zora Hurston in a letter to the Florida Department of Education, March 7, 1958.

"She was a charming person. All the students loved her. But she had difficulty getting transcripts of her records from Barnard. She was criticized by some teachers, but this is to be expected." — Dr. Leroy C. Floyd, past principal of Lincoln Park Academy, now dean of students at Indian River Community College, Fort Pierce.

"The head of the employment service called. He said, 'There's a writer in town in a difficult position who needs a friend.' He said, 'Uh, uh, uh—she's black.' I said, 'That's all right.' Then, I got a call from Zora Neale Hurston! I was a great fan of hers." — Marjorie Alder.

Zora's chance meeting with Marjorie Alder offered her respite from her troubles. Mrs. Alder, a radio and newspaper journalist with a sophisticated manner and captivating emerald-green eyes, offered Zora a renewed taste of bygone glory.

Nearly 20 years after her meeting with Zora Hurston, Marjorie Alder sits in the breeze-cooled living room of her home and brings Zora to life for the listener.

As the conversation intensifies, it is easy to understand why this 70-year-old cosmopolitan, who recharges her youth with daily tennis workouts and also is quick on the serve with words, got along well with Zora Hurston.

As Mrs. Alder remembers, "The first afternoon Zora came over, it was like she was digging in an archeological site for something. After that, she blossomed out and was Zora."

Zora, in exotic clothing, a turban wound around her head, started coming to dinner at Mrs. Alder's riverfront home. "I'm in my Zulu mood tonight!" she would proclaim, to see what reaction it would create among Mrs. Alder's often conservative, white guests. It was a reprise of "Princess Zora" from the Fannie Hurst days, though Zora never complained that these meals were bitter.

After eating her fill, Zora would take all the leftovers, not to stock her own barren larder, but to entice the children of School Court to within listening range.

There, distributing the food somewhat in the manner of the disciples feeding the multitudes with the five loaves and two fishes, Zora would feed the children and "teach them to be proud as black people," Mrs. Alder relates.

As their relationship progressed, Zora told Mrs. Alder that she had been the victim of jealousies and innuendoes at Lincoln Park Academy. She said she had been "bored out of her mind" as a Pan Am librarian. She told of her unhappiness at not having been able to do "crusading" work at the *Chronicle.*

She had been renting a 28-foot square, green, concrete-block house at 1734 School Court, just off 17th Street, from Dr. Clem C. Benton, a local physician. The rent was only $10 a week, but now she had no money and no place to go.

Photograph by N.Y. Nathiri

Benton's Quarters, October 1990. Observers say, except for its paved street, the Quarters looks today much as it did in the late 1950s when Zora lived there.

And she was deeply involved in writing a book — a history of the Biblical Herod the Great whom she saw as a misunderstood hero.

Her dedication to this controversial idea was obsessive. She first had conceived of such a work in 1945, according to Hemenway who reports that Scribner's had rejected one Herod manuscript in 1955. The firm, he notes, also had rejected other, different efforts.

"She had researched (the city of) Caesarea Philippi to the extent it was a place she had lived," said Mrs. Alder.

But Zora was in dire straits. Something had to be done. Mrs. Alder informed Dr. Benton of Zora's plight and found him proud and happy to give the house rent-free to Zora and her hybrid terrier "Spot".

Dr. Benton, a handsome, light-brown man with silver-white hair, who declines to give his age and whose unlined face does not betray his secret, opens his healing hands wide in expressing his feelings about Zora Neale.

Everything about Dr. Benton is immaculate, from his crisp, white smock to his bright, pleasant office. Concerned eyes peering through glasses, stethoscope about his neck, he is a larger-than-life portrait of the fatherly GP.

He regrets the death and burial of Zora away from her home in Eatonville, and the condition of her grave. He regrets also that she did not live to impart more of her creative genius to him so that he could set down his own experiences and thoughts.

But most of all, one feels, he regrets the loss of a good, intellectual friend, a dynamic conversationalist who, he admits, was often so profound, "she lost me."

He speaks with pride of helping to support Zora Neale. "I considered it an honor to sit and listen at her experiences as a writer, how she could go in and analyze, her method of getting background."

A somber look dims the light of pleasant memory in his face. Happy remembrances have their price: nothing fills the niche in his soul once occupied by Zora Neale.

"She made a desk and bookshelves out of fruit boxes. We provided some furniture. The things that were precious to her were her typewriter, her trunkful of letters and her reference books. She spent her time at that typewriter. It had been a long time since she had published, and she had lost contact with the publishing houses." — Marjorie Alder.

"She had no furniture or lights. She had a lamp, a table. She typed using an orange crate, with cushions, for a seat. She had a small, kerosene oil stove to do her cooking. Her situation was because of a lack of management. I don't think the woman cared anything about money. I think she cared only about writing . . .

"I said, 'I wish I had as much sense as you have.' She said, 'You got more sense. I'm a genius; I can do only one thing. You're smart, you can make a living.' " — Dr. Benton.

"When we went down to see her in Fort Pierce, we said we'll get you a (better) place to stay. We went out and got a place and paid the first down. You know, she didn't move. She didn't want that. She didn't want luxury." — Mrs. Clifford J. Hurston.

The once-great author striving for reunion with her lost muse, continued to grind out page after page of her new manuscript. Finally, in the second half of 1959, she again felt it was ready.

Marjorie Alder was conducting a syndicated radio interview program at the time. It required her to travel to New York City regularly. Zora entrusted the first few chapters of the manuscript to Mrs. Alder and asked her to take it to the publishing houses. Zora was seeking an advance to help sustain her until the book was published.

Mrs. Alder agreed to hand-carry the manuscript pages to New York. Then, she sat down and read them. A sad realization came over her.

"It wasn't her," says Mrs. Alder. But, dutifully, she carried the pages to three major publishers. All three turned the book down.

But the *Atlantic Monthly* magazine, Mrs. Alder found, was interested in what the once-famous black writer might have to say about integration of schools, something much on the nation's mind in 1959, and invited submission of an article on that subject.

Marjorie Alder turned south toward home. She was in a quandary about what to tell Zora concerning *The Life of*

Herod the Great, but relieved the *Atlantic Monthly* had, at least, given her hope to carry home to her friend.

"I didn't know what to tell her, but before I got to the (School Court) house, Dr. Benton's receptionist called and said Zora was very ill but would not go into the hospital until she had seen me," Mrs. Alder says.

"I went to see her. She was lying on a cot. I tried to talk to her, but she couldn't understand much of what I was saying. I soothed her to get her to go to the hospital. I doubt very much if the manuscript was discussed. I may have told her I had left it with someone to read."

Mrs. Alder did, however, obtain from Zora the manuscript of an article she had written on school integration. Zora, as always, baffled and amazed — her mental and spiritual independence, her Republican conservatism and her black pride bristling.

Though in declining health, Zora continued to wear her hats.

The manuscript reflected the thinking, damned by Civil rights leaders, that Zora had expressed in a letter sent to the *Orlando Sentinel* in 1955, decrying integration because, she believed, it implied black schools and teachers were inadequate.

"It was a tremendous surprise if not a shock," Mrs. Alder recalls. "She was the first person to indicate to me that 'Black is Beautiful.' She thought Howard was just as good as Yale. She wanted all black kids to go to Howard and achieve their uniqueness. She believed the blacks had equal mental and philosophical resources they should develop as blacks.

There should be no prejudice, but there should be no mixing."

The article was not submitted. Graver things were happening in the life of Zora Neale Hurston. She had suffered a stroke.

Zora was admitted to Fort Pierce Memorial Hospital, Oct. 12, 1959, and transferred on Oct. 29 to the segregated Lincoln Park Nursing Home, operated by the St. Lucie County Welfare Agency.

Her physical and mental health were deteriorating rapidly; she could no longer "manage herself," in Dr. Benton's words. There had been warning signs, though Zora had tried hard to conceal them.

But, she was aging, and she bore more than 200 pounds on her weary frame. She was suffering, the records show, from "hypertensive heart disease," and C.E. Bolen recalls that she had a touch of arthritis in addition to her other miseries.

She had been failing for some time, Dr. Benton said. She had been admitted to the hospital for treatment Sept. 19, 1958, hospital records show, and had received welfare aid to purchase prescription drugs on May 12, 1959, and food, June 9, 1959, according to Grace McNeil, present St. Lucie County welfare director.

When Zora was transferred from the hospital to the nursing home, her speech was impaired and she had "lost coordination," Dr. Benton said.

During the three months she remained at the home, the final three months of her life, she was incapable of doing that for which she had sacrificed so much — she could no longer write.

It was, then, the end of Zora Neale Hurston, creative genius, though Death lingered at the doorstep a painful spell before entering Zora Neale's nursing home room.

"But just as black dark came on, a terrible fear came on her somehow, and something like a great wind struck her and hurled her into the water . . . The doctor came and said she had suffered a stroke. One whole side of her body was paralyzed, so when she tumbled over into the lake, she could not get out." — *Dust Tracks on a Road.*

"What need has Death for a cover, and what winds can

blow against him? He stands in his high house that overlooks the world. Stands watchful and motionless all day with his sword drawn back, waiting for the messenger to bid him come." — *Their Eyes Were Watching God.*

"I had to go to New York again, and when I came home, I got a call from the black funeral home. They said they had Zora's body and didn't have enough to bury her and what should they do?" — Marjorie Alder.

Zora Neale Hurston was pronounced dead on arrival at Fort Pierce Memorial Hospital at 7 p.m., an hour after sunset, Jan. 28, 1960 — anywhere from 52 to 69 years of age, depending on which of her listed birthdates one chooses to believe.

Even the hospital records quarrel with themselves, one holding that she was born Jan. 7, 1908 and another insisting she arrived Jan. 7, 1891.

And the tombstone, placed on her grave by writer Alice Walker in 1973, argues with *Time* magazine, as can readily be seen in the opening paragraphs of this article. *Time* also puts *Seraph* into the category of Zora's writing about blacks, further illustrating the general confusion over Zora and her life.

Perhaps she was 69 when she died. Mabel Hurston thinks so. Mrs. Moseley, who knew her as a contemporary and who was 69 the year of Zora's death, thinks so. One of her surviving brothers told Hemenway he thought she was born in 1891.

But, as Zora perhaps slyly noted of the character Janie in *Their Eyes Were Watching God*, "The worst thing Ah ever knowed her to do was taking a few years offa her age and dat ain't never harmed nobody." Indeed.

"I was a correspondent for the *Miami Herald* at the time. I wrote an article about her, with something of her background, and that she had died and didn't have enough money to be buried. It was picked up by the UPI, and the major publishing houses and all her bigtime friends sent donations. At her funeral, there were a great many people, with a sprinkling of whites." — Marjorie Alder.

"I'm so sorry. She was supposed to have been buried in

Eatonville. A man connected with Rollins was going to start a library (of her work) and arrange to have her body brought here. But we couldn't get the consent of one of her three remaining brothers . . . When Zora died, we were the only ones (of the family) at the funeral."—Mrs. Clifford J. Hurston.

"They dressed her (for burial) in a pale pink, fluffy something. She would have been holding her sides laughing." — Marjorie Alder.

And, so, Zora Neale Hurston, who had begun life on one dusty road, came to her resting place at the end of another Feb. 7, 1960, 10 days following her death. Years would pass and the wild weeds grow over her unmarked grave before the world again would note she had passed this way.

She remains largely unknown and unread. Her black friends lament that their children and children's children haven't even a nodding acquaintance with Zora.

The present, young occupants of 1734 School Court have never read the writing of the woman who struggled to create and survive within the walls of their dwelling.

It is a hard fate for the woman Hemenway considers "as important a writer of that era as Richard Wright." Zora is "a tradition-bearer for a world Afro-American view," Hemenway said when contacted at the University of Kentucky, where he is an associate professor of English.

Fate seemed determined to obliterate even the memory of her. Marjorie Alder barely managed to head off destruction of Zora's final manuscript and large collection of correspondence in what Mrs. Alder terms a "weird postlude."

Informed by a School Court neighbor of Zora that a "steamer trunk" filled with Zora's effects had gone to the nursing home with her, Mrs. Alder got a county judge to appoint her guardian of the material.

Patrick N. Duval, a black deputy with the county sheriff's department, was ordered to retrieve the trunk. Arriving at the nursing home, he gazed down its long, central hallway to see smoke rising outside the back door.

He hurried down the hall to discover, as he had feared, that the trunk and its contents were being burned. Grabbing a nearby hose, he extinguished the blaze, saving many of the papers, including the Herod manuscript.

As she, herself, wrote in *Their Eyes Were Watching God*, "To my thinkin' mourning oughtn't tuh last no longer'n grief."

One must remember she exulted in her knowledge she was part of nature, an atom of creation.

"I love sunshine the way it is done in Florida," she wrote for *Twentieth Century Authors*. "Rain the same way — in great slews or not at all. I am very fond of growing things; I shall end my days as a farmer if I have my way. I like displays of nature like thunder-storms, with Old Maker playing the zigzag lightning through His fingers."

"Her view of death? It was absolutely nothing," said Marjorie Alder. "She thought it was practically aboriginal, the fuss about funerals and graves. That (the grave) has nothing to do with Zora."

Thus, the stranger contemplating her unscythed, nearly invisible grave in Fort Pierce may feel, as did Lucy in *Jonah's Gourd Vine*, "Ah got somethin' in mah heart ain't got no name" and hear the sound of "O-go-doe, the ancient drum . . . O-go-doe, the voice of Death" played in the hearts of the mourners for John Pearson in the same novel, but . . .

. . . one also knows the overwhelming sensation of spiritual triumph that Zora Neale shouted in bold voice in *Dust Tracks* and her deep-down, unswerving conviction that, while death might be hard, it was by no means final.

Reading her impassioned words, it grows easy to believe we can see Zora Neale alive and strong everytime the zigzag lightning veins the sky over Park Lake and the wind busies the oak limbs.

And knowing her love of and hope for the black children of School Court and a thousand other dusty lanes, one also feels she must lie content beneath the nodding weeds within sight and sound of the baseball-playing children, who know, at least, that hers is the grave of a "book-writer."

Graveyards, after all, are for the living, not the dead. They are places where we place on public display our emotions, our guilt and even our indifference.

Zora bristled but she did not fret. She had a faith in the natural workings of the universe, a faith that surmounted divisions of color, religion, culture, whatever, a faith she expressed clearly, forcefully, with beautiful simplicity in *Dust Tracks on a Road:*

"When the consciousness we know as life ceases, I know that I shall still be part and parcel of the world. I was a part before the sun rolled into shape and burst forth in the glory of change. I was, when the earth was hurled out from its fiery rim. I shall return to the earth to Father Sun, and still exist in substance when the sun has lost its fire, and disintegrated in infinity to perhaps become a part of the whirling rubble in space. Why fear? The stuff of my being is matter, ever changing, ever moving, but never lost; so what need of denominations and creeds to deny myself the comfort of all my fellow men? The wide belt of the universe has no need for finger-rings. I am one with the infinite and need no other assurance."

by N.Y. Nathiri

Access to a broad range of sources is essential if one is to paint a portrait inclusive of the subtleties and nuances of a complex person like Zora Neale Hurston. The broad-brush strokes of Zora's life in Fort Pierce are easy enough. There, she lived a hand-to-mouth existence. She survived, in large part, because of the largesse of others; she no longer possessed the writing prowess of her earlier years. She died the ward of St. Lucie County. The bold strokes paint a tragic picture, indeed.

But a well-executed portrait should also contain fine, delicate brush strokes to refine light and dark, or express subtleties in color. If one is to get an insightful glimpse into Zora's life in Fort Pierce, the community in which she lived must be afforded more than token consideration.

Black Fort Pierce of the late 1950s existed within certain boundaries and possessed a definite character. "Once you crossed the other side of canals, very deep ditches, with little water but thick foliage, you were automatically in white territory," remembers Cynthia Hart Scales, who grew up there.

"It was easier to count the number of paved streets because most of the roads in our section were unpaved," recollects Marjorie Alexander Williams, whose family owns Sarah's Memorial Chapel, the mortuary that buried Zora.

U.S. Highway 1 ran straight through the heart of the black business district, Avenue D. Here, every kind of retail operation, some owned by whites — grocery, dry cleaners, restaurants, theater, taxi, gas stations — served the needs of Fort Pierce's African-American community.

Orange groves and tomatoes were the chief sources of income for this community of about 5,000. Thirty-five cents a box, 20 boxes a day, meant weekly earnings of $42 (people didn't work on Sundays). The season ran from September to May. At $168 a month, the average annual income for more than 60 percent of Zora's community was $1,512. When the season was over in Fort Pierce, the bulk of this population followed the crops "up the road."

Those who didn't have to move to survive either worked for whites in menial positions or provided services to the African-American community. Dr. Clem Benton was the physician; Dr. Young, the dentist; Mr. Bolen, the newspaper publisher; "Lawyer" (Bill) Benton. The Peeks and Stones owned funeral homes. There were lots of churches. The faculty and staff at Lincoln Park Academy, where children in grades one through twelve were taught, completed the roster of the community's professionals.

This is Lincoln Park Academy, where, for a brief time, Zora was a substitute teacher.

Photograph by N.Y. Nathiri

Though it was financially poor, black Fort Pierce was rich in community pride and caring. Lincoln Park Academy, the school customarily referred to as that "segregated public school" where Zora taught for a time as a substitute teacher, had a faculty which saw to it that Fort Pierce's black children were prepared to go on to college or to work upon graduation. Yes, segregation meant hand-me-down textbooks and school supplies, or no school supplies at all, for Lincoln Park Academy students, but segregation could not prevent teachers from teaching. So, if St. Lucie County did not provide these students with frogs to dissect in biology, one of the community's morticians brought in an embalmed cat so the teacher could instruct the class.

Similar inventiveness could be found in every aspect of the curriculum, whether the lesson called for expertise in sewing or secretarial science. Marjorie Alexander Williams remembers her commercial course preparation was so thorough that when she graduated, not only did she know how to use her office machine, she could also take it apart, clean and reassemble it. She smiles when she says, "Our teachers did not play!"

As Fort Pierce's African-American community demonstrated its commitment to quality education, so, too, the community showed its caring for one another. Samuel Gaines, 18-year veteran school board member, recalls that traveling preachers knew they "just had to get to Fort Pierce" where they were guaranteed a meal at his grandfather's cafe. It was not unusual for guests to be at his family's dinner table.

Others easily recall instances of community sharing: Discovering a woman whose husband had abandoned her and their five children, a good Samaritan made sure the family received food and blankets and free medical care. This was the close-knit community into which Zora moved in the autumn of 1957.

Majorie Alexander Williams helped gather information on Zora's years in Fort Pierce. She is the granddaughter of Percy S. Peek, owner of Peek Funeral Chapel where services for Zora were held.

Only a few — whose roots also went back to Sanford — knew she was a famous author. This was true for C.E. Bolen, the publisher who hired her; Dr. Clem Benton, her landlord, and Rev. Albert Stone, in whose home she occasionally visited. A few others, like Margaret Paige, secretary at Lincoln Park Academy, also knew Zora was a famous author, and though now, an unkempt person, still keenly intelligent.

Margaret Paige, like Bill Benton, her neighbor, and Barbara Minus Wells, one of the children Zora befriended in her Benton's Quarters neighborhood, remembers the beautiful flowers Zora had in her front yard. She took great pride in them. Even then, it was clear to both woman and child that Zora was special.

Margaret Paige recalls wanting to understand how a woman of Zora's stature could be living as she was. She had been in her home; Zora had nothing and she dressed with little care. In fact, it was, in part, her style of dress that caused parents to caution their children about hanging around her. Zora did not dress in the '50s style; she wore loose-fitting house dresses, bandanas on her head, big slides on her feet, and no brassiere!

But Zora was captivating; she could tell about so many fascinating experiences — not in a boastful manner, but in a friendly, sharing way. Yes, Barbara Minus Wells knew Zora was strange, but that didn't stop her from chatting with "Miss Hurston." A girl of eight or nine, she and her friend, J.B. Chambers, used to fly kites in the Benton's Quarters' fields. She remembers one summer complaining about the heat and "Miss Hurston" replying that when she finished her book, she would build a swimming pool at the Quarters so the children would be able to keep cool.

As Zora declined, there were certain ones she could count on to help her. Though she walked everywhere, C.E. Bolen, her former employer, would take her to the grocery store whenever she indicated a need and buy her whatever she wanted. She could count on a meal at the Stones' home; it was not that she was a "regular," for it was not her way to seek charity. And Zora could count on Margaret Paige.

From all accounts within black Fort Pierce, it was Margaret Paige who was Zora's benefactor, in life and death. Helen Hughes, a teacher at Lincoln Park Academy, recalls Margaret Paige visiting daily with Zora as she was experiencing ill health, finding out what assistance she needed, returning to the teachers at Lincoln Park and soliciting their help. It was Margaret Paige, who, upon finding out that her neighbor, Peek Funeral Chapel (now Sarah's Memorial Chapel), was holding Zora's body and that she was about to be buried as a pauper, informed her community of the situation and raised the necessary funds for a funeral.

Samuel Gaines, himself a mortician, pretty much summarizes the community sentiment about Zora's burial and Margaret Paige's role in the final arrangement when he says: "Zora was not buried as a pauper. If she had been, her body would have been dumped in a box, and that would have been that. Margaret Paige was the person who got the teachers at Lincoln Park and others to donate so Zora could have a funeral."

Courtesy of the University of Florida Library

Zora, the consummate storyteller, relaxes with friends and neighbors.

Only in recent years have the people of Fort Pierce begun to feel the impact of Zora's having been among them. Barbara Minus Wells says she didn't realize that her "Miss Hurston" was who she was until she made the connection in 1985 after reading Alice Walker's *In My Mother's Garden*.

Increasingly, those who have been identified as having had first-hand knowledge of Zora find themselves the objects of interview requests. Some of them no longer respond because of their reluctance to be in the spotlight. There are accounts of people having been misquoted, misinterpreted or misused by the media. Margaret Paige, in fact, said to this interviewer, "I had to think a little bit about talking to you. I get calls all the time. People pass through; they get what information they can; and I never hear anything back from them.

"Several years ago, I did some general cleaning and threw out all the things I had left connected with the funeral. I didn't realize keeping them would be all that important. I had only been trying to do a good deed."

That willingness to do her a good deed probably best described Zora's relationship with her Fort Pierce community. To do her a good deed, not because of who she might have been, but because some saw her need; to extend to her charity, but not in an offensive manner. A little more than a decade before, Zora had suffered a horrendous blow at the hands of one of her own; the response to the false allegations shocked and traumatized her. Twelve years later, at the close of her life — and just afterwards — Zora's community responded to her with compassion.

Reunion

The James Weldon Johnson Collection, The Yale Collection of American Literature, Beinecke Rare Book Manuscript Library, Yale University

Zora was an environmentalist before it became fashionable.

R E U N I O N

▼

by N.Y. Nathiri

On Saturday, September 22, a rainy fall afternoon at Bradley International Airport in Hartford, Connecticut, Zora Neale Hurston's closest living relatives — her nieces and nephews — gathered for an interview. This would be the first time that Hurston family members, as a group, had consented to discuss their famous relative. All of them, save one, remembered Zora; each had met her and knew her in a different way; each would recount anecdotes to add to the body of information on her.

The opportunity to talk about Zora, to represent themselves, was important to these Hurstons. Zora Mack Goins, 65, is afraid to fly. It was the main reason she had not traveled to Eatonville for the festival honoring her aunt. She consented to fly from Brooklyn for this interview. Vivian Hurston Bowden, 54, had had a bicycle accident, and had been off work a week because of the pain. She traveled from Florida fortified by a knee brace, a walking cane and wheelchair. Winifred Hurston Clark, 70, had to catch a 6 a.m. flight from Nashville to make the 12:30 rendezvous. She had been awake since 1:30 that morning to make sure she didn't miss her flight. Dr. Clifford Hurston, Jr., 52, an Arizona State University administrator, crisscrosses the country often and was in the midst of a heavy travel schedule. He had completed a trip just a few days earlier but felt this excursion back to the East Coast was necessary. Hartford resident Edgar Hurston, 68, helped make contact with his sister, Winifred, and his cousin Zora, to ensure the date would work for all. And Lucy Hurston-Hogan, 33, who lives in Bloomfield, Connecticut, and who speaks professionally about her aunt's

contributions and legacy, adjusted her speaking schedule to
be present.

The afternoon was a time of coming together, of becoming
acquainted, of reestablishing family cohesiveness. Vivian
Bowden knew only her brother, Clifford. She had never met
any of her first cousins. Clifford had met Winifred, Edgar and
Lucy for the first time at the Hurston Festival.

Over a leisurely lunch, the relatives shared personal
information and family stories. By midafternoon, the time
had come for Zora's relatives to speak for the record.

From the beginning, it was clear that they were glad at last
to be able to speak for themselves. They seemed very much
aware of the negative image that surrounded Zora's family.

In her autobiography, *Dust Tracks on a Road*, Zora, herself,
indicates that her mother's death not only destroyed the
family's cohesiveness but also left her without that special
force to nurture her individual yearnings. Her mother, Lucy,
had urged her to "jump at de sun." She had granted her
daughter permission to be that quirky little girl who would

Photograph by N.Y. Nathiri

Zora's closest living relatives all had memories of their aunt to share during the "Reunion" interview.
(left to right) Winifred Hurston Clark, Dr. Clifford J. Hurston, Jr., Lucy Hurston-Hogan, Edgar Hurston,
Vivian Hurston Bowden and Zora Mack Goins.

Zora's nephew, Dr. Clifford J. Hurston, Jr. found this picture of his Aunt Zora (far right) in yet another hat. Family members are not certain of the identities of the other two.

Courtesy of Dr. Clifford J. Hurston, Jr.

while away her time daydreaming or engage passersby in easy conversation, even accompanying them down the road a piece.

When Rev. John Hurston quickly remarried, he brought into the Hurston home a woman who systematically ridded herself of the unwanted stepchildren. Zora was forced to move "from pillar to post" among relatives whose first priorities did not allow for her individual needs. With the death of her mother, Zora lost her emotional sustenance as well as the comfort and protection of a stable home environment.

Others writing about her life essentially affirmed the image of Zora as being estranged from her relatives, and in her final days, she is depicted as abandoned, alone, uncared for, even by her blood kin when she most needed them.

Almost immediately, Vivian Bowden addressed these sore points surrounding Zora's relationship with her family. Of her death and burial in Fort Pierce — generally characterized as a time when Zora was alone, sick and finally buried in a pauper's grave — she recalled:

"We visited her there (Fort Pierce) because we got a call

that she was sick. And we went down, my mom, my dad, and myself. I drove . . . And we asked her if everything was okay.

"She said she was fine; this is where she wanted to be. Dad offered her money and we went out and bought some things for her. She gave everything we bought to all the patients in the place. She didn't want them. She didn't want anything from anybody.

"Dad said, 'You have everything in order?' And she says, 'Well, when I die, the state is going to bury me. I don't want a penny from anybody and I will not accept it.'

"And that's why every time I read about how she died, it's very irritating to me. Because I was there and I heard. I was 19 and I know what she said. That's the way she wanted to go. She said she came in the world with nothing and that's the way she wanted to leave."

This photograph is a reconstruction of a portrait of Zora's parents, the Rev. John Hurston and Lucy Potts Hurston.

Courtesy of Winifred Hurston Clark

Vivian Bowden recalled another instance when her father and aunt were in touch. Of a visit with Zora in Eau Gallie, Florida, in the late '50s she remembered:

"She (Zora) looked fine. I remember her being very stout. She had on a house dress; was very proud of her yard. I remember the time we drove up, the odor of the sulfur from the stream that she had on the left side of the house. It was sulfur water and she explained about the minerals and everything in it. And then she took us through her house, which was very tiny.

"Mostly she got Dad on the side. And they talked. I have no idea what they talked about; they did a lot of communication, but I have none of the letters and I don't know what happened to them."

Courtesy of Lucy Hurston-Hogan

Zora's father, Rev. John Hurston, strikes the same pose with Zora's stepmother.

Zora Mack Goins and Winifred Hurston Clark also shared memories that shed a different light on Zora's relationship with her family. In 1933, Zora Mack, a child of eight, lost her mother, Sara, to pneumonia. Sara was Zora Neale's elder sister, and when her niece and namesake was left motherless, Zora brought the little girl to live with her in Harlem on 116th Street and Lenox Avenue. Zora Mack Goins smiled as she spoke of that time:

"She bought me the most gorgeous clothes. I never had beautiful things like that, but she liked nice things, and she was very nice to me . . . I stayed with her a while until my

Courtesy of Edgar Hurston

Zora's brother, Dr. H.R. Hurston, was a successful Memphis physician.

father remarried . . . I believe that's when Aunt Zora left and went to Haiti."

In the late 1930s, Zora again assumed the role of loving aunt by taking in her nieces after they had graduated from high school. Her eldest brother, Dr. Robert Hurston, a physician in Memphis, had also died in 1933. His widow had returned to teaching and was shouldering a large responsibility. Zora first brought Wilhemina and then Winifred to live with her in Eatonville at her Tuxedo Junction home. Winifred Hurston Clark recollected:

"She was really good to live with. She was interesting. And she stood her ground. People didn't run over her. And whatever she thought, she'd express it and you take it or leave it. I remember what good fried fish she cooked, and cole slaw; I'll never forget that. I just enjoyed living with her."

By family accounts it is clear that Zora had an ongoing positive relationship with members of her family. To be sure, the relationship was not the stereotypical family get-together for holidays and christenings.

Courtesy of Edgar Hurston

Wilhemina Hurston was Dr. H.R. Hurston's wife.

Even so, from what her nieces and nephews recalled, Zora's brothers and sisters accepted her for who she was and recognized "her ways."

Indeed, her nieces and nephews confirmed two images so often associated with their aunt: her unpredictability and her wandering. When asked if their parents counted on hearing from Zora during her many travels, they responded in unison, "Uh-uh. No." Her niece, Winifred, remembered from her elementary school days:

"She would come to visit us in Memphis. But there were times she would never tell us when she was coming . . . she would just pop up. Just like everything else . . . when I was living in the house in Eatonville. All at once she would say, 'I'm going to New York' and she would just get ready and go to New York and be gone two or three days."

Courtesy of Winifred Hurston Clark

Dr. Hurston poses with his three children, (left to right) Winifred, Edgar and Wilhemina.

Clifford Hurston, Jr. concurred:

"Dad talked about her because the family wrote . . . He'd say, 'Who knows where Zora may be . . . Zora may be in Africa, she may be in Alabama, she could be in California. She's a wanderer.' "

An ordinary person, their Aunt Zora was not; but just how did her relatives view her?

Vivian Bowden responded:

"I felt as though I had somebody very outstanding in my family because I remember when she came to Birmingham. I don't know whether she told them she was coming or not. All I know is I came home and there she was . . . I knew she had to be good because during the '40s, blacks didn't go to all-white universities to lecture. And during the '50s, you know, I lived in Birmingham so, you know, you didn't even walk on the sidewalks during that time. At night, you were in the middle of the street and hoping to get home safely . . . She came to lecture (at Birmingham Southern), something on literature, and I think she stayed two or three days. So then I knew, you know, 'cause I remember going to high school and telling my classmates, 'Oooo, Aunt

Courtesy of Lucy Hurston-Hogan

Zora's youngest brother, Everette Hurston, Sr., her nephew, Everette, Jr., and niece, Zora Mack Goins, share a lighthearted moment.

Courtesy of Lucy Hurston-Hogan

Everette Hurston, Sr. was in his eighties when this picture was taken.

Zora's in town. She's famous . . . ' "

Edgar Hurston contributed:

"I remember when she came to Tuskegee to make that lecture, I felt very important. And I told everybody around there that my aunt was famous and it made me feel good, you know, proud of her. She stayed three or four days. I didn't see her no more after that (1941)."

Clifford Hurston, Jr.'s image of his aunt is multidimensional:

"I remember my Daddy was very thrifty. He was extreme and I laughed at him. 'Why are you doing that?' I'm the type of person that spends. And so all I could hear was that Zora

Courtesy of Dr. Clifford J. Hurston, Jr.

Zora's brother, Clifford J. Hurston, Sr. and his wife, Mabel, are the parents of Vivian Bowden and Clifford J. Hurston, Jr.

was the kind if she had it, she would give it away. She would give before she received.

"I always remember Daddy talking about 'Aunt Zora's got a houseboat.' The thing I could imagine was this huge yacht. I had never seen a picture of it. I always imagined her as a Hollywood star, you know, as someone that's untouchable. And you know, she was a figure of my imagination because I only saw her once.

"I remember talking with her. And I can remember one tale she told me. She says, 'I was driving this car and I was going down this road and this policeman stopped me. So I

Wilhemina Hurston poses in front of the offices of her husband and brother-in-law.

got into 'the nigger act' — that was the word she used; I remember that, I kind of stared — and she says the policeman says, 'Woman, girl, where are you going?' And she says, 'I'm going — (wherever she says she was going) — and he says, 'Did you see that stop sign back there?' She says, 'What stop sign? No. I didn't see a stop sign.' So he got her out of the car and walked her back to the corner and said, 'See that stop sign.' And she says, 'Oh?' She says he said, 'S-T-O-P. Stop.' She says, 'Thank you, sir; I'm so glad you told me what that was. You know, I've been driving all these years and I didn't know what that meant.'

"And so that's the story I remember the most. And at the time I believed her. Now after knowing her and reading all about her I wonder how much is true and how much is fantasy."

Lucy Hurston-Hogan recalled her father, Everette's, habit of collecting family memorabilia and his attention to the publicity his sister received:

"We used to joke Dad about being a pack rat. He kept everything, every scrap of paper. He wrote down names, dates, and places, everything he did, everything that was going on, as much as he knew about what the brothers and sisters and the nieces and nephews were doing. He shared a place with Zora for a while."

Winifred remembered:

"When he (Everette) was well, I went to his apartment. He just had Zora all over it."

Not only have Zora's nieces and nephews treasured her, but they reported their children also proudly identify with her.

A view of the Memphis storefront where Zora's brothers, Dr. H.R. Hurston and pharmacist B.F. Hurston, had their offices.

Courtesy of Winifred Hurston Clark

Courtesy of Winifred Hurston Clark

Zora's brother, John C. Hurston, was a butcher and grocery store owner in Jacksonville, Florida.

Vivian Bowden:

"Every time they (two children) have to do a report, it's usually on Aunt Zora. And they make sure everybody knows it."

Courtesy of Winifred Hurston Clark

A young Zora sits with her nieces, Wilhemina (upper left), Winifred (at her knee), and nephew, Edgar (on her lap) in Memphis.

Edgar Hurston:

"I have a daughter who teaches school. She teaches black history in her class; and in that she emphasizes Zora."

Lucy Hurston-Hogan:

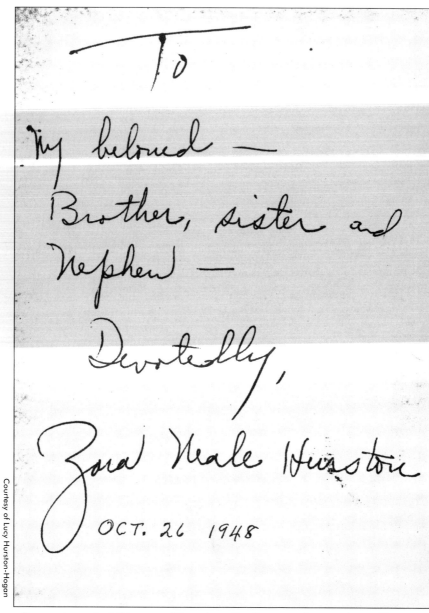

To

My beloved —
Brother, sister and
Nephew —

Devotedly,

Zora Neale Hurston

OCT. 26 1948

Courtesy of Lucy Hurston-Hogan

Zora autographed this copy of Seraph on the Suwanee *for members of her family. Everette Hurston passed this and other items he had collected on to his daughter, Lucy Hurston-Hogan.*

"Tony's read all her books. He has certain short stories that he writes, and that he does in school; reports, and stuff."

Perhaps Edgar Hurston summed up best the legacy of Zora:

"You couldn't help but learn something from her. When she talked, she'd always say something that would stick with you. She would make some kind of comment that you wouldn't forget. I loved her. She was just a nice person."

The interview had accomplished a number of things. First,

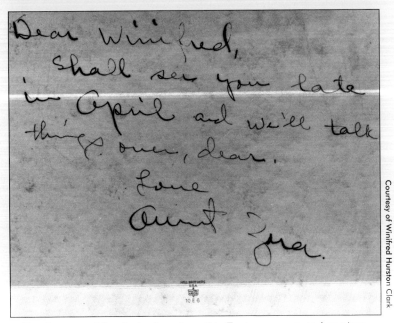

Zora's sense of family is clear from this Easter message to her niece, Winifred.

it had brought together Zora's closest living relatives. Meeting with one another, coming together in the name of family was a first-time occurrence for the six who journeyed to Hartford. These hours provided them an opportunity to sit together, remembering Zora, recalling their individual memories, while at the same time, contributing to a composite family view of their famous relative.

The interview allowed them to speak as family; to place on

PALLBEARERS

EUGENE C. WILLIAMS
LEROY C. FLOYD, SR.
ERNEST DICKERSON
D. C. FERNANDEZ
ROBERT JEFFERSON
LEMOYNE SARGEANT

FLOWER GIRLS

MEMBERS OF 12C CLASS
LINCOLN PARK ACADEMY

Anna Brown
Ora B. Long
Carolyn McAllister
Mary Price
Julia P. Lee
Ollie Richardson
Patreea Mitchell
Louise Roundtree
Corinne Slater

Funeral Rites

of the late

Zora Neale Hurston

Sunday, February 7, 1960 - 3 p. m.

Peek Funeral Chapel
724 Avenue D

Reverend Wayman A. Jennings, Sr.
officiating

Percy S. Peek Funeral Home
in charge

OBITUARY

Zora Neale Hurston was born in Eatonville, Florida, the first incorporated Negro town in America.

She attended Morgan College, Howard University, and Barnard College, receiving her degree from the latter. She received a fellowship from the Rosenwald Foundation in 1953, and Guggenheim Fellowships in 1936 and 1938.

Miss Hurston was one of America's foremost women authors. Her short stories and articles have appeared in OPPORTUNITY, STORY, EBONY and TOPAZ, and the SATURDAY EVENING POST. Her works, which were largely from folk sources, include "MULES and MEN," "JONAH'S GOURD VINE," and "THEIR EYES WERE WATCHING GOD."

She has worked in many capacities. At one time she was amanuensis for Fannie Hurst, noted novelist. She served as drama coach at North Carolina College for Negroes; as a principal speaker at the annual Boston Book Fair; as a librarian in the Library of Congress and at Patrick Air Base, Cocoa, Florida; and as a substitute teacher at Lincoln Park Academy, Fort Pierce, Florida.

Her personal life was as the fragrance of a beautiful rose, and her influence will ever live in whatever places she has resided. She was quiet in her manner and pleasant toward every one. To use her own words:

"I love courage in every form. I worship strength. I dislike insincerity, and most particularly when it vaunts itself to cover up cowardice. Pessimists and grouches, and sycophants I do despise."

This gathering today is evidence of the deep friendships formed by the deceased during a relatively short space of time.

Large was [her] bounty, and [her] soul sincere.
Heaven did a recompense as largely send:
[She] gave to misery all [she] had, a tear;
[She] gained from Heaven ['twas all [she] wished] a friend

ORDER OF SERVICE

PROCESSIONAL—

SELECTION .... "Nearer My God To Thee"

PRAYER .... Rev. H. W. White
Minister Friendship Baptist Church

SOLO .... Mrs. L. W. Haibe

SCRIPTURE .... Rev. R. J. Cliffin
Minister Mt. Olive Baptist Church

SELECTION .... "Just A Closer Walk With Thee"
Lincoln Park Academy Chorus

REMARKS .... Mr. C. E. Bolen
Publisher Chronicle

SOLO .... "He'll Understand and Say Well Done"
Betty Williams

REMARKS .... Principal Leroy Floyd, Sr.
Lincoln Park Academy

RESOLUTIONS AND ACKNOWLEDGMENTS OF CARDS,
LETTERS and TELEGRAMS .... Mrs. Paulyne Williams

EULOGY .... Rev. W. A. Jennings, Sr.
"Life in the Past, Present, and Future"
Minister St. Paul A. M. E. Church

A copy of the funeral program for Zora's burial

the record accounts of times past, which clearly alter the perception that Zora and her relatives were estranged from one another, non-communicative, non-caring. The interview also began a reuniting process.

The Hurstons acknowledged they had not been a close-knit family; there had been differences; but as Lucy Hurston-Hogan said, "Those differences occurred a long time ago; I wasn't even born; and I don't intend to let them stand in our way now." These first cousins having now met together decided to gather together their children so they can all meet each other. This generation of Zora's relatives seemed dedicated to strengthening family ties.

From the spirit that permeated the meeting room that September afternoon, it would be difficult to believe that all present hadn't known each other well for a number of years. The warmth and ease of conversation belied the facts.

After the interview ended, Lucy offered, "Today, it was as if Zora had reached back from the grave to bring us together again." It seemed so.

Celebration

The James Weldon Johnson Collection, The Yale Collection of American Literature, Beinecke Rare Book Manuscript Library, Yale University.

Zora packed a pistol for folklore gathering assignments.

Anything We Love Can Be Saved:
The Resurrection of Zora Neale Hurston and Her Work

by Alice Walker

The First Annual Zora Neale Hurston Festival
Eatonville, Florida
January 26, 1990

My first visit to Eatonville was on August 15, 1973, seventeen years ago. I was 28, my daughter Rebecca, 3. Sometimes she tells me of the pain she felt in childhood because I was so often working, and not to be distracted, or off on some mysterious pilgrimage, the importance of which, next to herself, she could not understand. This trip to Eatonville, not one of whose living inhabitants I knew, represented such a pilgrimage, one that my small, necessarily stoic child would have to wait years to comprehend.

But at the time, I felt there was no alternative. I had read Robert Hememway's thoughtful and sensitive biography of Zora Neale Hurston, after loving and teaching her work for a number of years, and I could not bear that she did not have a known grave. After all, with her pen she had erected a monument to the African-American and African-AmerIndian common people both she and I are descended from. After reading Hurston, anyone coming to the United States would know exactly where to go to find the remains of the culture that kept Southern black people going through centuries of white oppression. They could find what was left of the music; they could find what was left of the speech; they could find what was left of the dancing (I remember wanting to shout with joy to see that Zora, in one of her books, mentioned the "moochie," a dance that scandalized — and titillated — the elders in my community when I was a very small child, and that I had never seen mentioned anywhere); they could find what was left of the work, the people's relationship to the earth and to animals; they could find what was left of the orchards, the gardens and the fields;

they could find what was left of the prayer.

I will never forget, reading Zora, and seeing for the first time, written down, the prayer that my father, and all the old elders before him, prayed in church. The one that thanked God that the cover on his bed the night before was not his winding sheet, nor his bed itself his cooling board. When I read this prayer, I saw again the deeply sincere praying face of my father, and relived my own awareness of his passion, his gratitude for life, and his humbleness.

Nor will I forget finding a character in Zora's work called Shug. It is what my "outside" grandmother, my grandfather's lover and mother of two of my aunts, was called. It is also the nickname of an aunt, "Malsenior," for whom I was named. On any page in Zora's work I was likely to see something or someone I recognized; reading her tales of adventure and risk became an act of self-recognition and affirmation I'd experienced but rarely before.

Reading her, I saw, for the first time, my own specific culture, and recognized it as such, with its humor always striving to be equal to its pain, and I felt as if, indeed, I had been given a map that led to the remains of my literary country. The old country, as it were. Her characters spoke the language I'd heard the elders speaking all my life. Her work chronicled the behavior of the elders I'd witnessed. And she did not condescend to them, and she did not apologize for them, and she *was* them, delightedly.

It was very hot, my first visit to Eatonville. As hot in Florida as it had been in Jackson, Mississippi, where I lived, which I'd left early that morning, and where my small daughter remained, in the care of her father and her pre-school teacher, Mrs. Cornelius. I thought of her, as Charlotte Hunt and I drove about Eatonville and, later, Fort Pierce, on our mission. I wanted to mark Zora's grave, so that one day all our daughters and sons would be able to locate the remains of a human mountain in Florida's and America's so frequently flat terrain.

Today, knowing as I do the vanity of stones, their true impermanence, the pyramids notwithstanding, I would perhaps do things differently, but at the time my passionately held intention to erect a reminder of a heroic life indicated the best that I knew. And we were successful, I think, Charlotte Hunt and I, for we lifted the pall of embarrassment at our people's negligence off ourselves. We acted for Zora, yes, but in a way that relieved the shame of inactivity from ourselves. Paying homage to her, memorializing her light, her struggle and her end, brought us peace.

At least it brought me peace. I should perhaps not attempt to speak for Charlotte, who volunteered to be guide and companion to me. And yet I felt that Charlotte, too, loved Zora's spirit, and was no less concerned than I that her body not seem to have been thrown away.

But what is a dead body, what are bones, even of a loved one? If you mixed Zora's bones with those of Governor Bilbo's, for many years an especially racist oppressor of black people in Mississippi and psychologically of the whole country, the untrained eye would not be able to tell them apart. And nature, in its wisdom, has made sure that the one thing required of all dead things is unfailingly met. That requirement is that they return to the earth, which in fact, even as living bodies, they have never left. It matters little, therefore, where our bodies finally lie, or how and whether their resting places are marked — I speak now of the dead, not of the living who have their own needs and project those onto the dead — for our ultimate end, blending with the matter of the earth, is inevitable and common. I hope, myself, to become ash that is mixed with the decomposing richness of my compost heap, that I may become flowers, trees and vegetables. It would please me to present the perfect mystery of myself, prior to being consumed by whomever, or whatever, as rutabaga or carrot. Sunflower or pecan tree. Eggplant.

The spirit, too, if we are lucky, is sometimes ground to ash by the trials of life and tossed on the collective soul's compost heap. That is what has happened to what we have come to know as Zora. That is why we are here today, honoring her; startled perhaps by the degree of nourishment each of us has gained from her, startling in our diversity.

Zora Hurston's ash was diamond ash.

Diamonds, you know, start out as carbon, or coal, deep in the folds of the earth. Over eons enormous pressure builds up and crushes the coal into diamonds, the hardest crystals known. Then some of us, like Zora, are crushed further, by the lies of enemies and the envious hostility of friends, by injustice, poverty and ill health, until all that is left is diamond ash. For many years now, thanks to Robert Hemenway, thanks to Mary Helen Washington, thanks to Charlotte Hunt, thanks to Sherley Anne Williams, thanks to feminist and womanist scholars around the world, and thanks to millions of readers, Zora's diamond ash, her spirit, has been blowing across the planet on the winds of our delight, our excitement, our love.

And this is only right; it is the universe's justice. And it proves something that I think many of us here very much needed to see proved, twenty-odd years ago, when the commonest comment about Zora was the question Zora Who?: that love and justice and truth are the only monuments that generate ever widening circles of energy and life. Love and justice and truth the only monuments that endure, though trashed and trampled generation after generation. We have, together, accomplished the resurrection of Zora Neale Hurston and her splendid work, and can now tell our children what we have learned from this experience. Our children who are by now grown up enough to fly off on mysterious pilgrimages of their own. We can say with conviction that anything that they love can be sheltered by their love; anything they truly love can be saved. First in their own hearts, and then in the hearts of others. They have only to make their love inseparable from their belief.

We can tell them that on the day that we love ourselves, and believe we deserve our own love, we become as free as any earthbeings can ever be. And that we begin to see that, though our forms may differ, as an oak tree differs from a pine, we are in fact, the same. Zora is us. That is why, reading her, we smile or cry when she shows us our face.

I will close with this prayer which Zora collected, perhaps hoping that when black people read it, it would evoke for them one of the most longed for and truest images not only of the African-American face, but of the African-American psyche. For like all spiritually authentic peoples our ancestors understood that they did not need to be taught how to pray; that prayer, like poetry and music, of which it is mother, creates itself out of the lived experience, the pain and passion of the human heart. Typically, when poor black people sank to their knees, they created not a Lord's prayer, but a People's prayer.

I always weep when I read this, so bear with me.

"...You have been with me from the earliest rocking of
my cradle up until this present moment.
You know our hearts, our Father,
And all de range of our deceitful minds.
And if you find anything like sin lurking
In and around our hearts
Ah ast you, My Father, and my Wonder-workin' God
To pluck it out
And cast it into de sea of Fuhgitfulness
Where it will never rise to harm us in dis world
Nor condemn us in de judgment.
You heard me when Ah laid at hell's dark door
With no weapon in my hand
And no God in my heart,
And cried for three long days and nights.
You heard me, Lawd.
And stooped so low
And snatched me from the hell
Of eternal death and damnation.
You cut loose my stammerin' tongue;
You established my feet on de rock of salvation
And yo' voice was heard in rumblin' judgment.
I thank Thee that my last night's sleepin' couch
Was not my coolin' board
And my cover
Was not my windin' sheet.
Speak to de sinner-man and bless'im.
Touch all those
Who have been down to de doors of degradation.
Ketch de man dat's layin' in danger of consumin' fire;
And Lawd.
When Ah kin pray no mo';
When Ah done drunk down de last cup of sorrow

▼

Look on me, yo' weak servant who feels de least of all;
'Point my soul a restin' place
Where Ah kin set down and praise yo' name forever
Is my prayer for Jesus sake
Amen and thank God.

Anticipation had been building for months. The first ZORA! billboard proclaiming a festival in Eatonville, piqued curiosity. "Zora who?" "In Eatonville? Really!" "Wow, look at those colors." The bright billboard promised Energy! Entertainment!

As word spread about who would be at the first Zora Neale Hurston Festival of the Arts, the level of excitement rose to fever pitch. The guest list was impressive: author Alice Walker, actress Ruby Dee, story teller Augusta Baker, Zora's literary biographer Robert Hemenway and Ruth Sheffey, founder of the Zora Neale Hurston Society, were all coming to Eatonville.

Time whizzed by. There was much to be done. Booths to build, equipment to set up, an exhibit to mount, packets to stuff, tables and chairs to unload, tents to pitch. Would the volunteers be able to get it all ready in time?

Thanks to plenty of hard work and dedication, January 24 found Eatonville all dressed up and ready for company. ZORA! flags and Town of Eatonville flags lined Kennedy Boulevard, the town's main street. Bedecked with banners, the Denton S. Johnson Community Center welcomed visitors. The Wymore Career and Education Center, the festival's host facility, resplendent with its manicured landscape and tidied appearance, greeted the thousands who visited.

And the citizens of Eatonville? They were all wearing expressions of pride; anxious to be of whatever assistance they could be to the town's guests who had traveled from as far away as New York, Boston and Chicago to take part in the celebration of Zora Neale Hurston's life.

And the visitors? It was apparent that a great many of them

felt as if they'd died and gone to heaven. They were actually in Eatonville, *Zora's* Eatonville. And they were finding that, yes, indeed, the community was special.

Everything was festival perfect. The days went without a hitch. The crowds were constant; the level of intensity high, spirits charged. When January 27 came too soon and good-byes had to be said, the wonder of the weekend was that tiny Eatonville's celebration of Zora had caught the attention of the entire nation.

ZORA! and Eatonville town flags lined the streets and festival grounds (above). A ZORA! banner marked the entrance to Eatonville (left).

Eatonville's elected officials and town staffers, January 1990, posed for this group picture. (left to right) Merrile Glover, Councilwoman; Ada J. Sims, Vice Mayor; Eddie Cole, Councilman; Alvin B. Jackson, Mayor's Assistant; James Williams, Mayor; Louise M. Franklin, Secretary.

The Association to Preserve the Eatonville Community, Inc. (P.E.C.) dedicated the Zora Neale Hurston Memorial in honor of Eatonville's most famous citizen. Pictured are: Stephen C. Wright (podium), host of ceremonies; (right to left) Ruthenia Moses, Hurston Memorial Co-chair; N.Y. Nathiri, festival director; Lucy Hurston-Hogan, Zora's niece; Clifford J. Hurston, Jr., Zora's nephew; John L. Mica, Hurston Memorial Co-chair.

ZORA NEALE HURSTON
EATONVILLE'S DAUGHTER
1890 - 1960
ANTHROPOLOGIST, FOLKLORIST, WRITER
"SHE JUMPED AT THE SUN"
THE ASSOCIATION TO PRESERVE THE EATONVILLE COMMUNITY, INC.
JANUARY 26, 1990

Courtesy of P.E.C. / Photographs by Everett L. Fly

Courtesy of P.E.C. / Photograph by Everett L. Fly

Along with hundreds of others, Lucy Hurston-Hogan, Zora's youngest niece, and Clara V. Williams, former resident of Eatonville and retired school teacher, attended ceremonies dedicating Zora's Memorial.

Children enjoyed playing with balloons provided by C&S Bank, one of the festival's corporate underwriters.

Courtesy of P.E.C. / Photographs by Everett L. Fly

Jimmie Lee Harrell made soap the old-fashioned way.

Courtesy of P.E.C. / Photographs by Everett L. Fly

Artists treated browsers to colorful displays of jewelry and crafts native to Africa.

Decorative West African gourds were a popular festival item.

Photograph by Robert Goynes

Volunteer Tina Beacham painted the face of this youngster in the "Children's Corridor."

This vendor catered to festival-goers' appetite for some down-home cooking.

Courtesy of P.E.C. / Photographs by Everett L. Fly

As his family members looked on, Edgar Hurston talked to the local media about his famous aunt and the festival honoring her. (left to right) His daughter, Vickie Riley; his daughter, Joyce West and her daughter Crystal; his sister, Winifred Hurston Clark; his daughter, Fay Hurston.

Louise Thompson Patterson, who worked briefly with Zora and Langston Hughes, toured the grounds in a golf cart.

Photographs by Robert Goynes

Madison's Dolls delighted festival-goers with a variety of dolls from around the world.

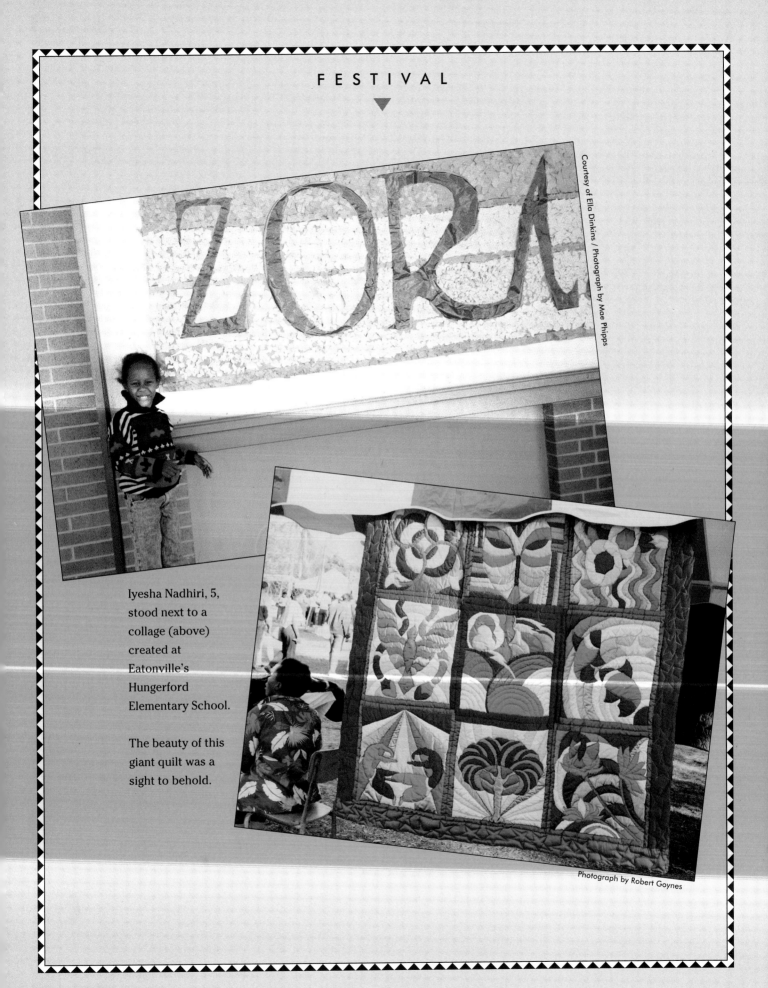

Iyesha Nadhiri, 5, stood next to a collage (above) created at Eatonville's Hungerford Elementary School.

The beauty of this giant quilt was a sight to behold.

Orlando artist Ron Kelly painted this portrait of Zora as a stamp. P.E.C. has nominated Zora to be commemorated on a U.S. postage stamp.

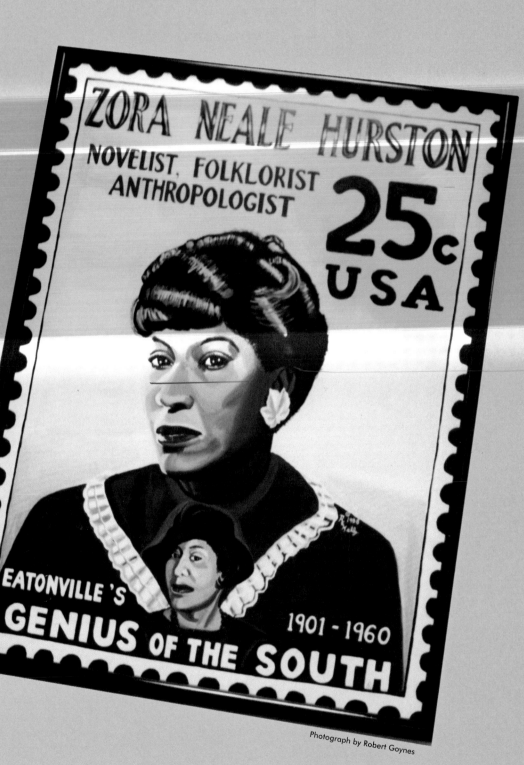

ZORA NEALE HURSTON

NOVELIST, FOLKLORIST ANTHROPOLOGIST

25c USA

EATONVILLE'S GENIUS OF THE SOUTH

1901 - 1960

Photograph by Robert Goynes

Artist Ron Kelly's interpretation of Zora and her Eatonville themes captured attention.

This portrait of Zora by Central Florida artist Curtis Deloney was a real eye-catcher.

Photographs by Robert Goynes

Actress Ruby Dee (above) enjoyed the banquet where author Alice Walker (right) shared her thoughts about Zora.

Photographs by Robert Goynes

▼

Courtesy of P.E.C. / Photographs by Shirley Cannon

Zora's niece, Lucy Hurston-Hogan, and her nephew, Clifford J. Hurston, Jr., paused between festival sessions for this picture.

Zora's nephew, Edgar Hurston and his family gathered for this group picture. (left to right) Karen Henderson, Edgar Hurston's daughter; Edgar Hurston, Winifred Hurston Clark, his sister; Fay Hurston, his daughter; Tammy Henderson, his granddaughter; Paul West, his grandson; Vickey Riley, his daughter, holding Crystal West, his granddaughter; his son Gregory Hurston; and his daughter Joyce West.

The
Neale Hurston
Festival

Courtesy of P.E.C. / Photographs by Ted Hollins

Pulitzer Prize-winning
author Alice Walker
greeted the audience
and then read a
passage that holds
special meaning
for her.

Veteran actress of
the stage and
screen, Ruby Dee
delighted festival-
goers with her
interpretive
reading.

Courtesy of P.E.C. / Photographs by Ted Hollins

Robert Hemenway, Zora's literary biographer, Ruby Dee and Lucy Hurston-Hogan, Zora's niece, shared the experience.

Ruby Dee signed ZORA! programs for all who came as festival director N.Y. Nathiri looked on.

Courtesy of P.E.C. / Photograph by Shirley Cannon

St. Lawrence A.M.E. Church, Eatonville's oldest house of worship, opened its doors to the crowd to show original murals donated by artist André Smith.

I·REST·IN·GREEN·PASTURES·MY·HEAD·ON·HIS·ARM
THE·LORD·WILL·PROTECT·ME·AND·KEEP·ME·FROM·HARM

Courtesy of St. Lawrence A.M.E. Church / Photograph by Frank Busby

Courtesy of St. Lawrence A.M.E. Church / Photograph by Frank Busby

U NDERSTANDING

▼

by Eleanor Mason Ramsey and Everett L. Fly

W hile it might appear that Eatonville was the highly original dream of one individual or a small group of individuals, the fact is the founding of Eatonville was representative of a historic phenomenon within America's chronicle. The "race colony," the name given to independent, planned communities intentionally comprised of members of African descent, first appeared on the American scene during the 19th century. Data related to the emergence of the race colony as a distinct political and social form are, at best, scant; thus, it is difficult to determine how many were formed.

Eatonville was the first incorporated municipality in the United States founded by settlers of African descent.

Overview

There are miscellaneous accounts of race colonies having been established in various regions of the United States. The heaviest concentration appears to have been in the Midwest and South with some having been

prominence. Some were towns of

with a mayor or commission form of government.

Their social organization was rooted in voluntary associations that cross-cut kinship ties. The colonies were essentially extended families. Education, then religion were the two most important institutions in the colonies. As a general rule, their charters set aside a section of land within the tract for an educational facility. These sections can be identified on subdivision maps by place names like College Heights in Taft, Oklahoma, and University City in Langston, Oklahoma.

Almost without exception, race colonies were situated in predominantly rural counties on undeveloped land, procured from private individuals, the federal government or the railroads. The land made available for African-Americans, as a rule, was of extremely poor quality, in terms of soil, water and physical accessibility. In those instances where the adverse conditions were overcome, it was only through a concerted group effort, and success was not without great travail in every case.

Origins

Race colonies emerged as a result of extreme racial hostility and violence. Their beginning dates back to slavery, where from the earliest records, they become the means with which African-Americans came to own land, secure an education, obtain political independence, and thereby enjoy the rights of full citizenship.

The race colony's role in black America's effort to gain full citizenship varied during different periods of history. In the 19th century after emancipation, it was considered a practical

Hard work contributed to the success of black settlements around the country. This Eatonville family prepares for a day of labor in the groves and in the home.

Courtesy of Rollins College

means for ex-slaves to secure farmland and the ballot, and to develop their institutions in an environment of social and physical liberty. For a period during Reconstruction, land could be obtained in the South, making it unnecessary to migrate much further than a neighboring county to establish a race colony. Yet, by the end of the 1860s ex-slaves found it increasingly difficult to locate cheap land in the South for group settlement. As Reconstruction drew to a close, race colonization was characterized principally by movement out of the South.

By the turn of the 20th century, the role and goals of the race colony had essentially been redefined. With their westward movement, the founders of these communities broadened their view of what they could accomplish. Still concerned with securing the recognition, respect and power that the all-black town would give them, these pioneers now broadened their mission to include changing the sentiments of whites toward African-Americans. Through education, moral and intellectual advancement, they believed African-

Americans living in towns they controlled could change race relations in America.

Development

The Reconstruction Period after America's Civil War (1867-1877) and the Great Exodus of 1879 mark the two historical periods when the largest number of race colonies were established. Reconstruction inaugurated social, if not

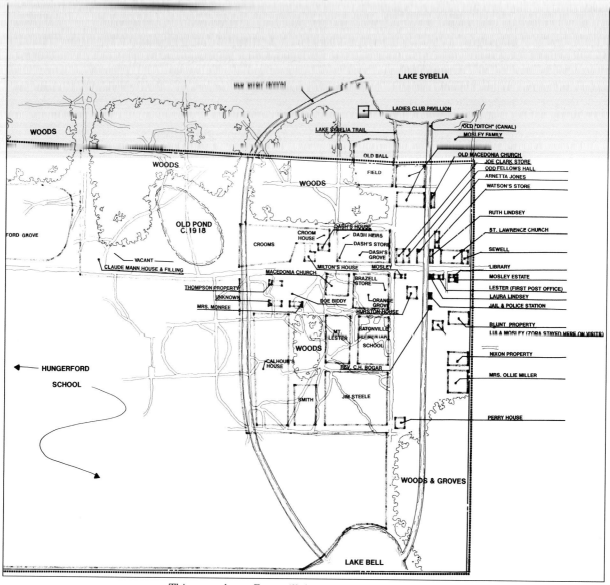

Courtesy of the Town of Eatonville

This map shows Eatonville's corporate limits in 1920.

economic reordering of Southern life; African-American men granted the right to vote used enfranchisement to look after their own economic interests. To the extent that their interests clashed with those of whites, the two groups collided. As Southern whites recaptured the reins of power (what they called "Redemption"), African-Americans looked to the race colony as the viable alternative. Having been generally distrustful of the Reconstruction administration from its beginnings, they had begun moving westward in the early 1870s as they saw Reconstruction being dismantled and as the federal government supported frontier expansion. With the election of 1876 and the infamous Tilden-Hayes Compromise formally marking the end of Reconstruction, African-Americans left the South in what is referred to as the Great Exodus of 1879.

Colonies Established During Reconstruction: Two Prototypes

Race colonies founded during this period share similarities in their political and social development. They were established most often because of the breakup of plantations

Courtesy of Harriett Moseley

This 1940s St. Lawrence A.M.E. Church choir carries on the spirit of worship that was the foundation of the church in 1882.

or large estates, when land usually was sold to former slaves who were eager to buy it.

Kendleton, Texas, located seventy-five miles southeast of Houston, exemplified acquisition of land through the breakup and sale of a plantation. Established in 1869, Kendleton, which remained unincorporated until 1970, was created from a nearly 1,600-acre tract sold to freedmen. Ben Williams, an African-American state legislator from nearby Colorado County, purchased the land from the 8,000-acre Kendleton plantation and resold it in 100-acre parcels for $1 an acre. Most of the 1,600 acres was swamp. Also during this same period, Jefferson Davis' ex-slaves bought acreage from his plantation on the lower Mississippi River near Vicksburg.

Under the leadership of Isaiah T. Montgomery (who later founded Mound Bayou, Mississippi), this colony became the second largest cotton producer in the state. But not for long. With the economic prosperity came political troubles and the pioneers soon found that as African-American land holders they had no certainty of title. In the early 1870s the freedmen's legal troubles with the Davis heirs began. The family claimed title to the land on grounds that were legally

Courtesy of Louise M. Franklin

Welcome to 1950s Eatonville. Cars line up in front of stores on Apopka Avenue, the town's main street.

dubious, but they nevertheless were successful in reacquiring the land and evicting the colony.

Incidents such as these continued to make African-Americans skeptical of their likelihood for success in the South.

Courtesy of Louise M. Franklin

Big Band greats Duke Ellington and Cab Calloway, blues man B.B. King, R&B king James Brown performed at Club Eaton during its heyday.

The Great Exodus

The times were ripe for movement. Although there is limited material on the subject, it does appear that the forty

Courtesy of Louise M. Franklin

A perfect example of the community continuum, the headquarters for the Association to Preserve the Eatonville Community is now in what used to be Mack's Garage where children could buy cookies, two for a penny.

years between 1870 and 1910 saw the greatest proliferation of race colonies in America's history. Numerous political factors influenced the migration. It was a period when the federal government was supporting the expansion of the western frontier. Early in 1870, Kansas was opened for homesteading. In 1890 Oklahoma Indian lands were appropriated and opened for settlement.

Throughout this period the railroads encouraged settlement on the rights-of-way the federal government had granted them on either side of their tracks. The rights-of-way, as much as ten miles on either side of the rail line, were vast tracts. These factors, complemented by the fact that the South was being inundated with pamphlets and agents encouraging African-Americans to migrate, set the stage for their "picking up their roots" to go elsewhere. All that was needed was the organizational skill to manage this Great Exodus. Benjamin "Paps" Singleton was one of the select few to fill this role.

Members of the Women's Auxiliary were Eatonville leaders who took great pride in their civic projects.

Courtesy of Ella Dinkins

Paps Singleton and Singleton Colony, Kansas

Paps Singleton established Singleton Colony in Kansas in 1873, settling there a group of colonists from the Nashville area. It was reportedly the first all-black settlement in Kansas and the first established on government lands. Singleton had begun his colonization effort in 1869 when,

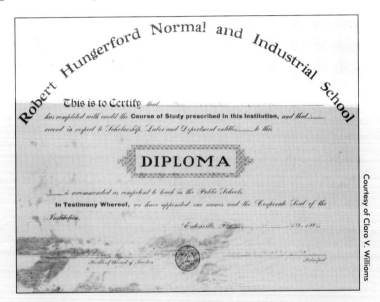

Courtesy of Clara V. Williams

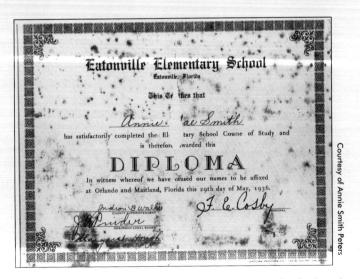

Courtesy of Annie Smith Peters

Education, then religion were the two most important institutions in these colonies. From its very inception, the Eatonville community placed great value on educating the young.

Mentioned in Zora Neale Hurston's Dust Tracks on a Road, *the Dash family (top) raised Mrs. Mary Montgomery (seated above). She and her daughter, Doris Bennett, still reside on the Dash family home site.*

with an itinerant preacher named Columbus Johnson, he formed the Tennessee Real Estate and Homestead Association to raise funds to purchase land in Tennessee for colonization.

Having formed the association, they encountered a major obstacle: Local land could be purchased only at exorbitant prices. Once that discovery was made, the members began their search for government lands. In 1872 an exploring party sent to Kansas returned with a favorable report. The next year Singleton, as president of the association, made a trip to Kansas. Pleased with his findings, he returned and organized 200 to 300 people, who migrated to Cherokee County in Kansas and formed the Singleton Colony. Through pamphlets and posters, Paps Singleton advertised the colony in every little Tennessee hamlet as an asylum for the recently freed slaves.

By 1881 Singleton was personally responsible

Courtesy of Harriett Moseley

Eatonville's mayor-council form of government also was found in other similar settlements. Mr. Lizzimore (above) was a longtime city council member in Eatonville.

for nearly one dozen other black communities in Kansas, some established directly by him and others inspired by his publicity and reputation. Associations similarly formed in other parts of the South also supported migration to Kansas. Unfortunately, little is known about the specific environmental conditions of the other Colonies inspired by Singleton. As a rule, land made available to colonists was on the western plains of Kansas, the site of the well-documented colony, Nicodemus. Although this region generally was considered too arid to support life, it typified the quality of land apportioned to blacks after the Homestead Act of 1860.

Paps Singleton was typical of the men who founded race colonies. Called "race men" because of their organized efforts to advance their race, they were called promoters and colonizers as well. It was they who had a vested interest in the colony's success, secured the land, negotiated the sales agreement, publicized the tract and, in many instances, even arranged transportation to the colony and lodging for the settlers upon arrival. In effect they were brokers, spanning the distance created by racism and politics to bring together white land sellers and African-American buyers.

Sports were integral to the Hungerford experience. These girls were on the basketball team.

Courtesy of Clara V. Williams

Edwin P. McCabe and Langston, Oklahoma

Almost 20 years after the founding of the Singleton Colony, nearly a dozen African-American communities were established in the Oklahoma Territory. They existed, however, in a political and social climate of extreme overt hostility. Appropriated Indian land, opened in 1889, was virtually unavailable to African-Americans by 1890. Local whites, with federal government support, were excluding, expelling and intimidating them from both established white communities and recently seized Indian lands.

Therefore, during this early period very few African-Americans acquired even the most uninhabitable government lands in Oklahoma. Land, when attainable, was chiefly acquired through private purchase directly from the railroads or from other freedmen of Indian ancestry. In some instances the railroad company actively promoted the idea of an African-American community in order to sell its holdings.

Langston, one of the earliest such communities established in Oklahoma, was founded in 1891. It was promoted by Edwin P. McCabe, formerly of Nicodemus, Kansas, who served as

Hungerford students applied the school's lessons in life to the classroom and to their chores.

In keeping with its working philosophy, the Hungerford School had its own sawmill.

state auditor of Kansas from 1883-1887. In 1890, he, together with a group of other African-American men, organized a migration to the Oklahoma Territory for the purpose of making it a Black State.

Given McCabe's political influence in his role as Langston's

Joe Clarke's vision brought Eatonville to life. This is a picture of him on the front porch of his home.

land developer and chief promoter, he was able to locate the town site adjacent to Indian lands. Although the tract was acquired through private sale, McCabe, acting as the colonists' broker, was later able to use his influence in the territorial government to make it possible for freedmen to secure additional Indian lands through homesteading.

In 1897, the same year McCabe was appointed auditor of Oklahoma Territory by Governor George Steel, the Oklahoma Territorial Legislature created a state educational institution for African-Americans, designated as the Colored Agriculture and

Reverend Haynes was a well-respected minister of St. Lawrence A.M.E. Church. He is shown in this June 1935 photo.

Candidate's Statement. Household of Ruth, No._____ G.U.

What is your name? {Mrs} {Miss} *Lula Hurston*

What is your age? *32* years _____ months

Where is your residence? *City of Eatonville Fla.*

Where were you born? *State of Ala*

Are you married? *yes*

What was your name before marriage? *Lula Poto*

Are you married to more than one man? *no*

Have you children? *yes*

Do your children enjoy good health? *yes as far as I know*

Are you sound in body? *no no far as I know* Are you subject to any periodical complaint which is liable to render you unable to follow your usual employment, or which is calculated to shorten life, and thereby render yourself and children a burden to this Household? *not as I knows*

Will you faithfully obey the laws, and submit to all the penalties that may be imposed, should it ever be proven that you have made a false statement? *I will*

Date, *Apr 26 1899* _____ (Let applicant sign here) Signed, *Lula Hurston*

Witness, _____ *F L Miller* W.R.

J E Clarke P.M.N.G.

Zora Neale Hurston's mother

Candidate's Statement. Household of Ruth, No. *443* G.U.O.O.F.

What is your name? {Mrs} {Miss} *Mrs Frances E. Jackson*

What is your age? *59* years _____ months _____ days

Where is your residence? *Eatonville, Fla*

Where were you born? *Lake City Fla*

Are you married? *no*

What was your name before marriage? *Slaughter*

Are you married to more than one man? _____

Have you children? _____

Do your children enjoy good health? _____

Are you sound in body? *as far as I know* Are you subject to any periodical complaint which is liable to render you unable to follow your usual employment, or which is calculated to shorten life, and thereby render yourself and children a burden to this Household? _____

Will you faithfully obey the laws, and submit to all the penalties that may be imposed, should it ever be proven that you have made a false statement? *yes*

Date, *June 10, 1968* _____ (Let applicant sign here) Signed, _____

Witness, _____ *Ossie Franklin* W.R.

Rachel Coker P.M.N.G.

Zora's mother, like many of Eatonville's civic-minded women, belonged to the Household of Ruth, a service organization dedicated to helping the needy. The club was active for more than 70 years.

Normal University of Oklahoma and built on forty acres donated by the townspeople. The town's economic base was effectively diversified through the location of a university within its environs. Langston is one of the few colonies that has remained viable, and its continuity must in no small way be attributed to McCabe's success in locating Oklahoma's first black college in the town.

FRIDAY, MAY 12, 1933
OPEN HOUSE

FRIDAY, MAY 12, 1933—2:30 P. M.
COMMENCEMENT EXERCISES

Processional

Negro National Anthem .... *Johnson*

Invocation

"Send out thy Light" .... *Gounod*
Chorus

"Robbing the Kitchen of its Drudgery" ....*Salutatorian*
Ida M. Harley

"Out on the Deep" .... *Lohr*
Leroy Curry

"Why I propose to study Agriculture" .... *Valedictorian*
Walter Jameison

"Lullaby" .... *Brahms*
Ida M. Harley

Commencement Address .... *Rev. R. L. Jones*
Pastor, Mt. Zion Baptist Church
Orlando, Florida

Presentation of Certificates and Awarding of Prizes

"My Task" .... *Ashford*
Chorus
Recessional

COMMENCEMENT
PROGRAM

of the

Hungerford
Vocational School

EATONVILLE, FLORIDA

MAY 7-12, 1933

L. E. HALL, *Principal*

SUNDAY, MAY 7, 1933—4:00 P. M.

BACCALAUREATE SERVICES

Sermon .... *Rev. J. A. Finlayson*
Pastor, Mt. Pleasant Baptist Church
Orlando, Florida

MONDAY, MAY 8, 1933—8:00 P. M.
ORATORICAL CONTEST

TUESDAY, MAY 9, 1933—8:00 P. M.
PIANO RECITAL
Admission 10 cents

Juanita .... *Spanish Melody*
Danny Boy .... *Weatherly*
Chorus

March .... *Presser*
Two Waltzes .... *Presser*
Flossie Lawson

The Water Nymphs Waltz .... *Spaulding*
Mary Johnson

Asleep in the Deep .... *Petrie*
Leroy Curry

A Lively Dance .... *Matthews*
Edna T. Harley
Lula M. Baldwin

Little Snowman .... *Felton*
Jarvie Johnson

Four Leaf Clover Waltz ....*Engelmann*
Ella A. Johnson

Hungarian Dance ....*Engelmann*
Vivian Hall

Twilight Hour .... *Grey*
Henry M. Clifton

By the Waters of Minnetonka ....*Lieurance*
Ida M. Harley

I am a pirate .... *Pitcher*
Edna T. Harley

Hallowe'en March .... *Parlow*
Minuet in G .... *Beethoven*
Lula M. Baldwin

Song of the Volga Boatmen ....*Russian*
Men's Chorus

WEDNESDAY, MAY 10, 1933—8:00 P. M.
"THE ROAD TO THE CITY"
Play by the Graduating Classes
Admission 15 cents

A copy of the Hungerford School's 1933 commencement program.

There is much to learn about the cultural history of African-Americans from the race colonies. These all-black communities, though a little-known phenomenon in America's multiethnic society, provide a laboratory for

studying the roots of African-American associational
structures, political institutions and attitudes toward
education and world view. The race colony is a historic
social process that provides a window through which to
observe the continuities of African-American culture.

Eatonville, among its many contributions to African-

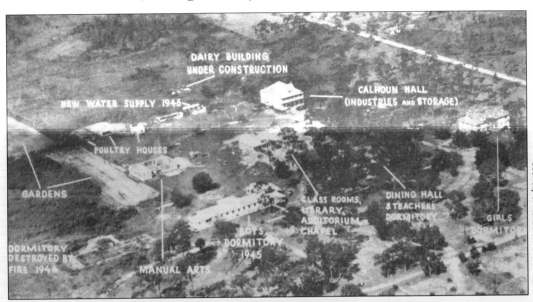

*This aerial view of the Hungerford Campus gives some clue to
the learning experiences available to the students.*

American cultural history, was a community founded in the
tradition of the race colony. Therefore, a reconstruction of its
early history offers a glimpse of this important aspect of
African-American culture within the American cultural fabric.

African-American settlers first came to the northeast
section of what is now called Orange County, Florida,
because of the work opportunities in Maitland, a town being
built by Northern whites, many of whom were Civil War
veterans.

Coming from neighborhoods and enclaves in the
surrounding counties and towns as well as from West Florida,
Alabama, Georgia and South Carolina, these African-
Americans provided the necessary work force to build a
town where whites never had lived. In 1885 Joe Clarke,
originally from Georgia, was the first African-American to
acquire land.

Maitland's civic, political and religious leaders helped

Clarke start Eatonville. Lewis H. Lawrence and Josiah Eaton were chief among Maitland's residents who believed that African-Americans should have the opportunity to buy land. The parcel that Lawrence deeded to the founders of the St. Lawrence A.M.E. Church and the property that Eaton sold to Joe Clarke were the physical beginnings of Eatonville.

Lewis Lawrence and Joe Clarke platted and subdivided the land they owned and filed their plans with the Orange County

Courtesy of St. Lawrence A.M.E. Church

In 1882, New Yorker Lewis H. Lawrence deeded land to Joe Clarke and other members who founded St. Lawrence African Methodist Episcopal Church, five years before the town of Eatonville was incorporated.

clerk's office. They then sold parcels to other African-Americans, and by 1887, there were enough individual landowners to file for the town's incorporation. August 18, 1887, is Eatonville's official birthday.

Lawrence and Clarke were community-oriented developers. They divided their land into lots large enough for a house and small farm with enough room for citrus trees, a vegetable garden or small animals. The lots were sold at prices working people could afford, and Lawrence and Clarke were careful to follow all the legal steps to plat and subdivide the land. This was very important because it allowed each property owner to have clear title and thereby made it easy for the land to be passed on to family and heirs. The succeeding generations respected this principle. Many of the original lot lines, street and town boundaries are still used today.

Two years after the town of Eatonville was incorporated, the Hungerford Normal and Industrial School was founded by Robert F. Hungerford. Russell and Mary Calhoun, the school's first and second principals, patterned the school after Booker T. Washington's Tuskegee Institute. The original campus was built on thirty-six acres of land.

The school was designed to teach students the work ethic,

Courtesy of Ella Dinkins

A.N. Johnson, a mayor of Eatonville in the '30s, carved this sign to direct people traveling to the Hungerford School.

sound moral and human values and the proper social graces. All students were required to live on campus for at least one term. They had to help with chores as Hungerford was equipped with barns, workshops, animal pens and gardens, all designed to allow the school to be self-sustaining.

Because the school and town started within months of one another, they naturally grew and changed together. Large amounts of land were available close to town for the school's agricultural programs. The school needed students and the town could supply them. The town and region wanted to be

Courtesy of Louise M. Franklin

St. Lawrence A.M.E. Church was a focal point in the development of the historic Eatonville community.

trained and educated. The school had the facilities and programs to meet the need. The school and town helped stabilize each other and increase chances of survival. Hungerford was a permanent place for learning and education. Eatonville was a permanent community and town. Hungerford taught discipline and values to future leaders of Eatonville. The community spoke out for the practical and political rights of the school.

Though initially separate from the Eatonville community, Hungerford was eventually annexed into the town. By the time of the annexation, the school had grown to include 304

This 1915 photo shows female students waiting to dine at Hungerford's Calhoun Hall.

acres, which accounted for 62 percent of Eatonville's area.

Citizens of the Eatonville community have an established tradition of community involvement and pride. Early on, women joined together for social welfare purposes — sewing quilts and sharing baskets of vegetables and other items that were distributed to the community's needy. The Household of Ruth had an Eatonville chapter whose records show an active membership spanning the late 1800s to 1968. Over time, members included Eatonville's most well-thought-of and/or socially prestigious women — wives of mayors, preachers, store owners.

As the town grew and its needs changed, the citizens' civic involvement kept pace. By the late 1950s, for example, Eatonville recognized its need to organize a volunteer fire department. Mr. Mack Robinson, longtime businessman and owner of Mack's Garage, became the first fire chief. The

Women's Auxiliary, whose membership roster included many of Eatonville's community leaders, formed immediately to support the men's efforts.

A constant of the Eatonville community has been its citizens' reservoir of civic pride. We see it initially with the twenty-seven founders in 1877. It continues at the turn of the century with the energy and dedication of the sewing circles and women's clubs. Zora's popularization of Eatonville and its culture mark high points for town pride. With today's efforts to place the town on the National Register of Historic Places and to develop it as a center for the popular study of African-American life and culture, Eatonville seems destined to hold on to its special heritage.

Eleanor Mason Ramsey holds a Ph.D. in cultural anthropology from the University of California at Berkeley. Her dissertation was on Allensworth, a community founded by persons of African descent. She was instrumental in having the town designated as a California state park. Dr. Ramsey is founder and president of Mason Tillman Associates in San Francisco.

Everett L. Fly is a licensed landscape architect, who for the past thirteen years has researched towns and settlements established by persons of African descent. He recently completed Eatonville's historic survey, the first step in the town's quest to be placed on the National Register of Historic Places. Fly has worked extensively with the National Trust for Historic Preservation in Washington, D.C.

by Thelma J. Dudley and N.Y. Nathiri

D
IALECT! For too many readers, the word conjures up all sorts of obstacles. Strang-luk'in' spillins, wi'er' punz-u'ashuns, har 'tuh un-neistan' meanins uh wurds. "Why in the world," they ask, "should I spend my leisure time struggling to decipher what I'm reading?"

It is true that Zora Neale Hurston uses dialect in her writing; and, at first glance, the words on the page may look incomprehensible, however, dialect need not be a hindrance to your enjoying some truly wonderful writing.

Every language has its dialects — combinations of sounds produced by a tongue not familiar with the standard language. Some dialects are more difficult to decipher than others: Donald McCallum of the St. Andrews Society of Central Florida gives these two examples of how dialect can look like a foreign language.

Try these Scottish variations:

It's a braw, bricht, moon-licht nicht. (It's a beautiful, bright lit, moonlit night.)

Ye're a'richt, ye ken. (You're all right, you know.)

Though people may share the same ethnic background, they still may have glaring differences in the way they speak their standard language. Also consider, as another example, whites from Appalachia and those from Brooklyn.

The dialects of African-Americans also vary, reflecting the culture of the region from which they come. For example, African-Americans from Charleston, South Carolina, speak differently than those from New Orleans or Thomasville,

Georgia. Charleston's cultural mix is predominantly Indian, African, and British; New Orleans', Spanish, French, and African; Thomasville's, British and African. This means that people from each of these locales pronounce the sentence, "they are going downtown" in three different ways.

From Charleston (Geechie or Gullah) — "De gwa downtown."
From New Orleans — "Dee gwon downtown."
From Thomasville — "Day goin downtown."

Your question then is: "Do I have to know the culture to read the dialect?" The answer is no. You can understand the dialect used by writers like Paul Laurence Dunbar, Langston Hughes and Zora Neale Hurston, even though spellings and punctuations may vary. What is the same is all their characters try to speak English as closely as possible to how they hear it. This is, in fact, the main idea to keep in mind when reading an African-American dialect: Read what you see, phonetically, and you will be able to understand the meaning. Try these examples to see how easily you can read and understand what's written.

From Paul Laurence Dunbar, one of the great poets of African descent, who wrote during the late 1800s and early 1900s:

SONG

Wintah, summah, snow er shine,
Hit's all de same to me,
Ef only I kin call you mine,
An' keep you by my knee.

Ha'dship, frolic, grief er caih,
Content by night an' day,
Ef only I kin see you whaih
You wait beside de way.

Livin', dyin', smiles er teahs,
My soul will still be free,
Ef only thoo de comin' yeahs
You walk de worl' wid me.

Bird-song, breeze-wail, chune er moan,
What puny t'ings dey'll be,
Ef w'en I's seemin' all erlone,
I knows yo' hea't's wid me.

From Langston Hughes, well-known 20th century African-American poet and writer:

MOTHER TO SON

Well, son, I'll tell you:
Life for me ain't been no crystal stair.
It's had tacks in it,
And splinters,
And boards torn up,
And places with no carpet on the floor —
Bare.
But all the time
I'se been a-climbin' on,
And reachin' landin's,
And turnin' corners,
And sometimes goin' in the dark
Where there ain't been no light.
So boy, don't you turn back.
Don't you set down on the steps
'Cause you finds it's kinder hard.
Don't you fall now —
For I'se still goin', honey,
I'se still climbin',
And life for me ain't been no crystal stair.

From Zora's *Mules & Men* (1951, Indiana University Press):

Once a man had two sons. One was name Jim and de other one dey call him Jack for short. Dey papa was a most rich man, so he called de boys to 'im one night and tole 'em, "Ah don't want y'all settin' 'round waitin' for me tuh die tuh git whut Ah'm goin ter give yuh. Here's five hundred dollars a piece. Dat's yo' sheer of de proppity. Go put yo'selves on de ladder. Take and make men out of yourself."

Though all of her major works contain some dialect, some of her books contain more than others. The people you'll encounter in *Jonah's Gourd Vine* and *Their Eyes Were Watching God*, and in the folklore collection, *Mules and Men*, are mostly African-American. Thus you will find dialect on almost every page. In her autobiography, *Dust Tracks on a Road*, her novel about Florida whites, *Seraph on the Suwanee*, and her folklore collection from the Caribbean, *Tell My Horse*, African-American dialect is not so prevalent.

Jez 'memba'; ya have no reazon tuh feel unsur'n 'bout readin' 'n unnerstannin de dialec spok'n by Africun 'maricuns. Jez read de sounz ya see; de wu'ds and dey meanin's be clar tuh ya.

Thelma. J. Dudley was a classroom teacher for more than fifty years, having initially ended her teaching career at Valencia Community College in Orlando, Florida. An active civic and religious worker, Dudley travels nationally and internationally on behalf of projects she represents. She recently returned full-time to the classroom as a doctoral student at the University of Central Florida.

by N.Y. Nathiri

Zora's books will appeal to a broad spectrum of readers: if you like adventure, Zora will keep you on the edge of your seat; if you prefer thorough, first-hand accounts of the bizarre, Zora will hold you spellbound; if you enjoy "folks' tales," big and little lies, Zora will keep you chuckling; if you want to ponder life's great questions, Zora will command your attention; if you are fascinated by books where the author's life intertwines with what she writes, Zora will captivate you; and if you just want to indulge yourself in what today, we'd call a "dime store, romance novel," Zora will allow you to pleasantly while away your time. You may not enjoy everything she has written; undoubtedly, you'll have your favorites. But it's hard to imagine that Zora won't hold your attention once you have given her a chance.

Jonah's Gourd Vine (1934) is said to be autobiographical. In part, it's a story of a man, too good-looking for his own good, his inability to resist the temptations of his flesh, and his utter dependence on his first wife, who clearly understands his limitations and consistently protects him from himself. Zora introduces us to people and places we'll encounter again in her later writing — John and Lucy, Eatonville, Sanford, Macedonia, Zion Hope, Polk County.

Why not see how Zora handles the notion, "behind every great man, there's a wo-man."

Different folks see things differently. *Mules and Men* (1935) serves up a rich slice of Americana unknown to America's reading public until she had collected this material. The book's two major parts, one on folk tales, the other on hoodoo, give a view of Southern life from the bottom. The folks comment candidly on servitude, add color to creation stories and provide Brer 'Gator, Brer Rabbit, Brer Dog and Sis Cat, among others, the opportunity to expound on "the why" of things. No Joel Chandler Harris adaptation here. Zora gives us the real McCoy.

In part two on hoodoo, Zora takes us through the paces of her first-hand experiences with magic. She is a serious researcher, making every sacrifice necessary to better understand her subject. You may need a seat belt for part two.

Their Eyes Were Watching God (1937) is considered to be Zora's best. The novel centers around Janie Crawford and her journey to find fulfillment. Zora is brilliant in her description of Florida's natural wonders, her analyses of personalities and her use of the dramatic. She gives you a beautiful sense of "wild and wooly Florida" of a half-century ago.

Though you may not have the time, you'll want to read this novel in one sitting.

Prepare yourself for *Tell My Horse: Voodo and Life in Haiti and Jamaica* (1938). Divided into three parts — Jamaica, Politics and Personalities of Haiti and Voodoo in Haiti — *Tell My Horse* is Zora's tour de force as a social commentator and as a field researcher. In both areas, she pulls no punches, providing you little time to catch your breath before leading you on to her next amazing experience.

If you are not accustomed to reading first-hand reports on voodoo, you should take certain precautions. Because Zora is not sensational in her reporting, you are going to encounter stomach-riveting accounts with little warning. If you like to eat while you read, consider suspending this habit when you begin *Tell My Horse.*

In *Moses, Man of the Mountain* (1939), Zora draws upon several traditions to tell the story of Moses and his fight to free the Israelites from Pharaoh and the Egyptians. Using psychoanalytical methods, Zora seeks to explain why this prophet of God acted as he did. Zora obviously is writing on several levels. If you are a student of the craft, you probably will enjoy following her as she tackles the challenges she has set for herself.

Though Zora calls *Dust Tracks on a Road* (1942) an autobiography, students of her life claim she took certain liberties with its style as well as its substance.

Generally, she writes in a breezy fashion, telling what she wishes of her life, editorializing as she sees fit on subjects ranging from vaudeville entertainers to race relations and world affairs.

If you have read some of her other work, you probably will recognize events and people who have appeared elsewhere. You may find yourself nodding knowingly as you piece together the information Zora provides. Or you may find what Zora writes raises even more questions than the explanations she offers.

Zora's critics say her last novel, *Seraph on the Suwanee*, (1948) is a major departure from her previous work because her central characters are Southern whites and because the book lacks the sparkle that so much of her other work possesses.

If you are troubled by a main character who feels herself a helpless emotional and physical slave of her husband; if you are bothered by African-American characters who seem to be comfortably stereotypic; if you prefer subthemes that are consistently developed, you probably will be disappointed with this work.

But before you throw up your hands in despair, take heart in the knowledge that Zora does toy in 1948 with issues that still perplex us today — development and its negative environmental impact, the sometimes cozy relationship between the criminal element and elected officials; the need for diversification of state economies.

If you can get a hold of a copy of *Seraph*, you might find it's been worth your investment in reading time.